D0902339

THE TOUR DE FRANCE
QUIZ BOOK

THE TOUR DE FRANCE QUIZ BOOK

JOHN DT WHITE

APEX PUBLISHING LTD

First published in 2005 by
Apex Publishing Ltd
PO Box 7086, Clacton on Sea, Essex, CO15 5WN, England

www.apexpublishing.co.uk

Copyright © 2005 by John DT White
The author has asserted his moral rights

British Library Cataloguing-in-Publication Data
A catalogue record for this book
is available from the British Library

ISBN 1-904444-35-0

Typeset in 10.5pt Times New Roman

Production Manager: Chris Cowlin

Cover Design: Andrew Macey

Printed and bound in Great Britain

This Book is dedicated to my Mum, Rosaleen Doherty White,
who bought me my first racing bike.

Thanks Mum.

FOREWORD

Reporting the Tour de France each July has been a way of life for me since 1973. It is, without doubt, the most fascinating sporting event of any year and, as you will discover in the excellent little book, it is an occasion which has developed a long history.

I am surprised it has taken so long before someone has produced a Quiz Book on La Grande Boucle, but now you have the chance to test your knowledge of the greatest bicycle race on earth. John White has spent many long hours researching this book, discovering little known facts and, in a fun way, now brings a transparency to the event many will never has seen before.

Over the thirty-three years I have been covering the race for both newspapers and television, there have been many changes. Henri Desgrange, the founder of the race when it was first held in 1903, could never have foreseen how popular the event would become in 2005.

Even in 1904 he was considering cancelling it because of bribery and sabotage, but it survived and now a cast of 4000, move with the race every day.

Well done, John, and you might like to know that Paul Sherwen and I will, in 2005, have covered 60 Tours between us. Now where exactly is that question in the book!

- Phil Liggett

FOREWORD

A Scary thought that Phil Liggett and I have covered 60 Tours between us (33 for him and 27 for me)!

The things that I love about commentating at the Tour is the little anecdotes and pieces of history that we have to dig up every year - that's what a lot of people tell me they find so fascinating.

Now that this quiz book has come out Phil & I will really have to be on our toes as a lot more people will have access to the quirky little stories and facts about the "greatest bike race in the World." Since I first rode the Tour in 1978 I have seen the race develop so much recently under the guidance of Jean Marie Leblanc who has been responsible for growing the race into what it is today but retaining it's much of it's folklore.

I hope you enjoy the book as much as I did and find a few interesting questions to catch out you friends. You might just get a chance to find out how far afield the race is followed- even in Africa they know the "The Tour de France". By the way, which King of the mountains winner by the way was born in Africa?
Answer - Richard Virenque was born in Casablanca!

- Paul Sherwen

INTRODUCTION

I have been a huge fan of the Tour de France since I first watched Channel 4's broadcast of the Greatest Cycle Race in the World during the 1980's. The physical limits, and pain, that those guys put themselves through over 3 weeks racing is simply staggering. Just riding a bicycle for 5 hours is hard enough but then when you see the speed they do it at, it is breathtaking. And what about the Polka-Dot Jersey Winners - The Kings of the Mountains? Just imagine riding a bike for 5 or 6 hours uphill, I cringe with pain just contemplating it. But it is feats such as the latter that make the sport so appealing and the riders household names and National Heroes.

Since Le Tour first began in 1903 there have been some marvellous duels between riders and some truly wonderful Champions. For many reasons, not least of all because an Irishman won it, I will always remember the 1987 Tour de France. I can still see Stephen Roche catching up with Pedro Delgado at the summit of La Plagne in the Alps. He was completely exhausted after putting in a super human effort that essentially clinched the Yellow Jersey for him that year. And what's more in 1987 Stephen also won the Giro d'Italia and World Road Race Championship. Or who will ever forget Greg LeMond's victory over Laurent Fignon in the 1989 Tour De France on the Champs d'Elysees by 8 seconds! I can still recall the look of disbelief on Laurent Fignon's face.

Many truly great riders have all won the Yellow Jersey - Fausto Coppi, Jacques Anquetil, Eddy Merckx, Bernard Hinault, Laurent Fignon, Greg LeMond, Miguel Indurain and the Greatest Rider of them all, the 6 times winner, Lance Armstrong. I have nothing but the deepest respect and admiration for Lance who fought back from cancer to win 6 consecutive Tours (1999-2004) and I would love to see him claim a 7th Yellow Jersey on the podium in Paris in July 2005.

So I hope this Book brings back as many wonderful memories for you as it has for me. In closing I would like to say thanks to all those people who were kind enough to supply pre-publication quotes for my book especially Chris Carmichael, Dave Duffield, Hennie Kuiper, Alex Stieda, Bob & Eddy at Tour Xtra, Cor Vos and Graham Watson.

I am also very grateful to John Miranda, Mark Schmisseur and Barry Quick for supplying the photographs for use in my book. My thanks must also go to Todd Carrier for supplying the "Liggettisms" and of course, to Phil for his wonderful race quotes.

Finally, what can I say about Phil Liggett & Paul Sherwen that would do them justice. I am honoured that Phil & Paul kindly agreed to write the Foreword for my book because for me they are "Le Tour". Phil & Paul have not only attracted a new audience to the Greatest Cycle Race in the World, they are outstanding Ambassadors for the Sport. Thank you both.

Yours in Sport,

John DT White

2004 - LE TOUR - 1

1. In what country did the 2004 Tour de France start?

2. How many Teams participated in the 2004 Tour de France - 19, 20 or 21?

3. Who won the 2004 Tour de France?

4. How many actual Stages were there?

5. How many riders started the 2004 Tour - 179, 189 or 199?

6. Which Stage was the longest - Stage 1, Stage 7 or Stage 10?

7. Who won the "King of the Mountains" jersey?

8. To the nearest 250km, how long was the 2004 Tour de France?

9. How many Flat Stages were there in the 2004 Tour de France - 9, 10 or 11?

10. To the nearest 3 km/h, what was the average speed for the Tour?

LANCE ARMSTRONG

11.   How many times has Lance won Le Tour?

12.   Including the 2004 Tour de France, how many Tour de France has Lance participated in - 9, 10 or 11?

13.   Can you name the rider who has finished Runner-Up to Lance on 3 occasions in Le Tour?

14.   When Lance took part in his first ever Tour de France, what mobile phone company-sponsored Team did he ride for - Motorola, T-Mobile or Telekom?

15.   How many times has Lance not been ranked in the overall positions at the end of a Tour de France?

16.   In what year did Lance win his first Tour de France?

17.   Name the Spanish rider who finished Runner-Up to Lance in the 2002 Tour de France.

18.   What part of Texas does Lance come from?

19.   In what year did Lance claim his first Stage victory - 1992, 1993 or 1994?

20.   How many times has Lance finished outside Le Tour's Final Top 5 positions?

KNOW YOUR NATIONALITY - 1

*ALL YOU HAVE TO DO HERE IS ASSOCIATE THE RIDER
WITH HIS NATIONALITY*

21.	Daniele Nardello	Danish
22.	Greg Lemond	Irish
23.	Fernando Escartin	French
24.	Bjarne Riis	American
25.	Stephen Roche	English
26.	Tom Steels	French
27.	Lauren Fignon	Spanish
28.	Chris Boardman	Italian
29.	Jacques Anquetil	Spanish
30.	Francisco Mancebo	Belgian

FASTEST TOURS

ALL YOU HAVE TO DO HERE IS ASSOCIATE THE WINNER AND YEAR WITH THE TOP 10 RANKINGS FOR THE FASTEST EVER TOUR DE FRANCE

31.	Lance Armstrong:	2002	1st
32.	Lance Armstrong:	1999	8th
33.	Miguel Indurain:	1995	7th
34.	Lance Armstrong:	2000	5th
35.	Marco Pantani:	1998	6th
36.	Bjarne Riis:	1996	2nd
37.	Lance Armstrong:	2003	4th
38.	Miguel Indurain:	1992	3rd
39.	Lance Armstrong:	2004	9th
40.	Lance Armstrong:	2001	10th

1960s TOUR WINNERS

ALL YOU HAVE TO DO HERE IS ASSOCIATE THE RIDER
WITH THE YEAR HE WON LE TOUR

41.	Lucien Aimar	1968
42.	Jacques Anquetil	1962
43.	Jan Janssen	1961
44.	Gastone Nencini	1963
45.	Jacques Anquetil	1960
46.	Felice Gimondi	1966
47.	Eddy Merckx	1969
48.	Jacques Anquetil	1965
49.	Roger Pingeon	1964
50.	Jacques Anquetil	1967

EDDY MERCKX

51.   What nationality is Eddy?

52.   How many times did Eddy win Le Tour?

53.   Name any year in which Eddy won Le Tour.

54.   In how many Tour de France did Eddy participate - 7, 8 or 9?

55.   Can you name the Dutch rider who finished Runner-Up to Eddy on 2 occasions in Le Tour?

56.   How many times was Eddy not ranked in the overall positions at the end of a Tour de France?

57.   Name the famous French rider who finished Runner-Up to Eddy when he won his last Tour de France.

58.   Apart from the Yellow Jersey, name any other overall classification Jersey that Eddy won in Le Tour.

59.   What was the highest number of Stages ever won by Eddy in a single Tour de France - 6, 7 or 8?

60.   How many times did Eddy win Cycling's World Championships?

FOREIGN STARTS FOR LE TOUR

*ALL YOU HAVE TO DO HERE IS ASSOCIATE THE COUNTRY
WITH THE YEAR LE TOUR STARTED THERE*

61.	Luxembourg	1987
62.	Holland	1982
63.	Belgium	1980
64.	Spain	1954
65.	Germany	2002
66.	Ireland	2004
67.	Switzerland	1958
68.	Belgium	1998
69.	Holland	1978
70.	Germany	1992

KING OF THE MOUNTAIN
WINNERS - 1

ALL YOU HAVE TO DO HERE IS ASSOCIATE THE RIDER WITH THE YEAR HE WON THE KOM TITLE

71.	Claudio Chiappucci	1970
72.	Richard Virenque	1977
73.	Tony Rominger	1985
74.	Thierry Claveyrolat	1986
75.	Bernard Hinault	1993
76.	Pedro Torres	1998
77.	Eddy Merckx	2004
78.	Christophe Rinero	1973
79.	Lucien Van Impe	1991
80.	Luis Herrera	1990

LE TOUR - 1

81.   In what year was the first Tour de France staged - 1901, 1902 or 1903?

82.   Who was Runner-Up in the 1987 Tour de France but came back the next year and won it?

83.   Can you recall the name of the last Italian rider to win Le Tour?

84.   In what Irish city did the 1998 Tour de France start?

85.   What colour of Jersey is awarded to the Best Young Rider in Le Tour?

86.   Who wore the No.1 Jersey in the 2004 Tour de France?

87.   What colour of Jersey does the leading rider in the King of the Mountains competition wear?

88.   In 1954, Le Tour did not start in France for the first time in its history. In what country did it start?

89.   In 1909, for the first time the winner of Le Tour was not from France. What country provided the Yellow Jersey winner - Holland, Italy or Luxembourg?

90.   Who has finished Runner-Up in Le Tour on 5 occasions since 1998?

JACQUES ANQUETIL

91. In how many Tour de France did Jacques participate - 8, 10 or 12?

92. In what year did Jacques participate in his first Tour de France - 1957, 1958 or 1959?

93. On how many occasions was Jacques not ranked in the overall positions at the end of a Tour de France?

94. How many times did Jacques win Le Tour?

95. Name any 2 of the years in which Jacques won the overall Yellow Jersey in Le Tour.

96. How many times did Jacques win a Stage in the Tour de France?

97. How many different riders finished Runner-Up to Jacques in a Tour de France?

98. For how many different Teams did Jacques win a Tour de France - 2, 3 or 4?

99. What was the first Team for which Jacques won a Tour de France?

100. What nationality was the rider who won Le Tour after Jacques' final victory?

2003 TOUR DE FRANCE

101. Who won Le Tour?

102. Can you name the American rider who finished in 4th place?

103. What Australian rider won the Green Jersey?

104. Name the French rider who won the "King of the Mountains".

105. Name the Italian rider who finished in 7th place overall?

106. What Russian rider was awarded the White Jersey for being the Best Young Rider in Le Tour?

107. What "Christophe" was the highest-placed French rider, finishing Le Tour in 8th position?

108. What Team won the Stage 4 Team Time Trial - AG2R, Quick Step or US Postal?

109. Name either of the 2 Euskaltel riders who finished in the Top 10.

110. Can you name the French rider who won Stage 20: Ville-d'Avray to Paris?

LUIS OCAÑA

111.   What nationality is Luis?

112.   In how many Tour de France did Luis participate - 7, 8 or 9?

113.   In what year during the 1960s did Luis participate in his first Tour de France?

114.   On how many occasions was Luis not ranked in the overall positions at the end of a Tour de France?

115.   In what year did Luis win his only Tour de France - 1973, 1974 or 1975?

116.   Can you recall the name of the French rider, and future winner of Le Tour, that finished Runner-Up to Luis in Q115?

117.   How many times did Luis win a Stage in the Tour de France - 9, 10 or 11?

118.   In what year did Luis claim his first Stage victory - 1970, 1971 or 1972?

119.   What is the highest number of Stages that Luis won in a single Tour de France - 5, 6 or 7?

120.   How many times has Luis finished in Le Tour's Final Top 5 positions - 1, 2 or 3?

LE TOUR RECORDS

121. What has been the smallest winning margin in Le Tour - 8 seconds, 18 seconds or 38 seconds?

122. Name either of the 2 riders involved in Q121.

123. Can you name the French rider who holds the record of 8 for most Top 3 placings?

124. Who was the British rider who set the fastest ever Prologue speed of 55.152 kph over 7.2km in 1994?

125. To the nearest 5 minutes, what has been the biggest winning margin in Le Tour's history?

126. Can you name the Italian rider who won Le Tour by the biggest winning margin?

127. What famous rider holds the record of 34 career Stage victories in Le Tour?

128. What is the highest number of Stages won by a rider in a single Tour?

129. Name any 1 of the 3 riders that share the record of Stage victories in Q128.

130. Name the Dutch rider, and former Tour de France winner, who holds the record of having participated in the most Tour de France with 16 between 1970 and 1986.

LE TOUR WINNERS BY COUNTRY

ALL YOU HAVE TO DO HERE IS ASSOCIATE THE COUNTRY WITH THE NUMBER OF TIMES ONE OF ITS RIDERS WON LE TOUR

131.	Italy	4
132.	Switzerland	8
133.	France	1
134.	Ireland	9
135.	Spain	2
136.	Holland	36
137.	Luxembourg	9
138.	Germany	18
139.	Belgium	2
140.	USA	1

BEST SPRINTER WINNERS - 1

*ALL YOU HAVE TO DO HERE IS ASSOCIATE THE RIDER
WITH THE YEAR HE WON THE GREEN JERSEY*

141.	Sean Kelly	1995
142.	Djamolidin Abdoujaparov	1979
143.	Eddy Merckx	2004
144.	Baden Cooke	1976
145.	Erik Zabel	1972
146.	Robbie McEwen	1989
147.	Freddy Maertens	2003
148.	Laurent Jalabert	1986
149.	Eric Vanderaerden	1999
150.	Bernard Hinault	1993

2004 TEAM LEADERS

ALL YOU HAVE TO HERE IS ASSOCIATE THE RIDER
WITH THE TEAM HE LED

151.	Lance Armstrong	Lotto-Domo
152.	Christophe Moreau	Rabobank
153.	Robbie McEwen	Quick Step
154.	Jan Ullrich	Crédit Agricole
155.	Michael Boogard	Euskaltel-Euskadi
156.	Iban Mayo	CSC
157.	Stuart O'Grady	US Postal
158.	Richard Virenque	Illes Balears-Banesto
159.	Francisco Mancebo	Cofidis
160.	Ivan Basso	T-Mobile

THE NEARLY MEN 1985-1994

ALL YOU HAVE TO DO HERE IS ASSOCIATE THE RIDER
WITH THE YEAR HE FINISHED RUNNER-UP IN LE TOUR

161.	Steven Rooks	1985
162.	Gianni Bugno	1986
163.	Greg Lemond	1987
164.	Claudio Chiappucci	1988
165.	Piotr Ugramov	1989
166.	Tony Rominger	1990
167.	Pedro Delgado	1991
168.	Laurent Fignon	1992
169.	Claudio Chiappucci	1993
170.	Bernard Hinault	1994

ROGER PINGEON

171. What nationality is Roger?

172. In how many Tour de France did Roger participate - 7, 8 or 9?

173. In what year during the 1960s did Roger participate in his first Tour de France?

174. What famous Belgian rider did Roger finish Runner-Up to in the 1969 Tour de France?

175. On how many occasions was Roger not ranked in the overall positions at the end of a Tour de France?

176. In what year did Roger win his only Tour de France - 1965, 1966 or 1967?

177. Apart from the Yellow Jersey, did Roger win any other overall classification Jersey in the Tour de France?

178. How many Stages did Roger win in Le Tour - 3, 4 or 5?

179. Apart from the year he won Le Tour, can you name any other year in which Roger won a Stage?

180. How many times has Roger finished in Le Tour's Final Top 5 positions - 1, 2 or 3?

TOUR WINNERS - 1

ALL YOU HAVE TO DO HERE IS ASSOCIATE THE RIDER
WITH THE YEAR HE WON LE TOUR

181.	Lance Armstrong	1961
182.	Miguel Indurain	1952
183.	Jacques Anquetil	1983
184.	Lauren Fignon	1987
185.	Eddy Merckx	1990
186.	Stephen Roche	1996
187.	Bernard Hinault	2003
188.	Greg Lemond	1979
189.	Fausto Coppi	1994
190.	Bjarne Riis	1974

THE RED JERSEY

191.   In what type of "Sprints Classification" did the Red Jersey use to indicate the leader of?

192.   In what year was the "Sprints Classification" referred to in Q191 first introduced - 1970, 1971 or 1972?

193.   Who won the first "Sprints Classification" title - Marc Demeyer, Pieter Nassen or Willy Teirlinck?

194.   What nationality is the rider in Q193?

195.   Can you name the Irish rider who won the most "Sprints Classification" titles?

196.   Name any year in which the rider in Q195 won the title.

197.   Name the British "Barry" who won the "Sprints Classification" title in 1974.

198.   In what year was the Red Jersey first introduced - 1984, 1985 or 1986?

199.   What nationality was the rider who was the first to wear the Red Jersey - Belgian, Dutch or Irish?

200.   In what year was the last Red Jersey won in Le Tour - 1989, 1990 or 1991?

MOST STAGE WINS IN LE TOUR

*ALL YOU HAVE TO DO HERE IS ASSOCIATE THE RIDER
WITH THE NUMBER OF STAGES HE WON IN LE TOUR*

201.	Jean Alavoine (France)	22
202.	André Leducq (France)	16
203.	Jacques Anquetil (France)	25
204.	André Darrigade (France)	19
205.	Eddy Merckx (Belgium)	17
206.	Nicolas Frantz (Luxembourg)	28
207.	François Faber (Luxembourg)	21
208.	Bernard Hinault (France)	20
209.	René Le Greves (France)	35
210.	Lance Armstrong (USA)	16

STEPHEN ROCHE

211.   What nationality is Stephen?

212.   In how many Tour de France did Stephen participate - 10, 11 or 12?

213.   In what year during the 1980s did Stephen participate in his first Tour de France?

214.   On how many occasions was Stephen not ranked in the overall positions at the end of a Tour de France?

215.   In what year did Stephen win his only Tour de France?

216.   Can you recall the Spanish rider who finished Runner-Up to Stephen in Q215?

217.   How many times did Stephen win a Stage in the Tour de France - 2, 3 or 4?

218.   In what year did Stephen claim his first Stage victory - 1984, 1985 or 1986?

219.   For what Italian Team did Stephen ride when he won the Tour de France?

220.   How many times did Stephen finish in Le Tour's Final Top 5 positions?

RUSSIAN RIDERS

221.   Can you recall the Russian rider who won his first Stage in the Tour de France in 1991 (Stage 20) and also won Stage 4 in 2004?

222.   Can you name the Russian who won Stages 19 and 22 of the 1991 Tour de France - Viatcheslav Ekimov, Dimitri Konyshev or Alexei Sivakov?

223.   This current Russian rider wore the White Jersey in his first Tour and then won the White Jersey the following year. Name him.

224.   This Russian rider participated in 4 Tour de France between 1991 and 1994 with his highest overall placing being 38th in 1992. Is he - Vladislav Bobrik, Alexei Sivakov or Dimitri Zhdanov?

225.   I took part in the first of my 4 Tour de France in 1995, and in 1996 I wore the Yellow Jersey and won a Stage. Who am I?

226.   Name the Russian rider who won the same Stage number in both the 2003 and 2004 Tour de France.

227.   How many times did Dimitri Konyshev win a Stage in Le Tour - 4, 6 or 8?

228.   This Russian rider participated in 3 Tour de France between 1998 and 2001 with his highest overall placing being 87th in 1998. Name him.

229.   Can you name the rider who took part in his first Tour de France in 1994, finishing in 52nd place, and did not enter the race again until 1998 when he was not ranked?

230.   Name the first Russian rider to win a Stage in the Tour de France.

TEAM TIME TRIAL WINNERS - 1

*ALL YOU HAVE TO DO HERE IS ASSOCIATE THE TEAM WITH
THE YEAR THEY WON THE TEAM TIME TRIAL IN LE TOUR*

231.	1982	Système 'U' (France)
232.	1984	Ariostea (Italy)
233.	1986	ONCE (Spain)
234.	1990	GB-MG (Italy)
235.	1991	Gewiss (Italy)
236.	1993	Raleigh (Netherlands)
237.	1995	Fiat (Belgium)
238.	2002	Panasonic (Netherlands)
239.	2003	Renault (France)
240.	1977	US Postal Service (USA)

TOUR JARGON

ALL YOU HAVE TO DO HERE IS ASSOCIATE THE WORD
WITH ITS PROPER MEANING

241.	Domestique	The yellow jersey worn by the leading rider in Le Tour
242.	Étape	The toughest climb in any Mountain Stage of Le Tour
243.	Maillot Jaune	The description for the route that Le Tour takes each day
244.	Parcours	The Manager of a Team in Le Tour
245.	Peloton	A rider who willingly sacrifices their own chances of winning Le Tour and works in every Stage to help their Team leaders
246.	Contre La Montre	A Team in Le Tour
247.	Tête de la Course	The Time Trial
248.	Hors Catégorie	The front of the race
249.	Équipe	The name associated with the main bunch of riders
250.	Directeur Sportif	A Stage in Le Tour

BERNARD THEVENET

251. How many times did Bernard win Le Tour?

252. Name any year in which Bernard won the overall Yellow Jersey.

253. In how many Tour de France did Bernard participate - 10, 11 or 12?

254. In what year did Bernard participate in his first Tour de France - 1970, 1971 or 1972?

255. On how many occasions was Bernard not ranked in the overall positions at the end of a Tour de France?

256. What famous Belgian rider finished Runner-Up to Bernard when he won his first Tour de France?

257. How many times did Bernard win a Stage in the Tour de France - 9, 10 or 11?

258. In what year did Bernard claim his first Stage victory - 1970, 1971 or 1972?

259. For what French car manufacturer-sponsored Team did Bernard ride when he won his first Tour de France?

260. How many times did Bernard finish as Runner-Up in Le Tour?

HISTORY OF LE TOUR

261. Can you recall the name of the sports magazine that was responsible for creating the Tour de France - L'Auto, L'Équipe or Le Velo?

262. What was the total prize money on offer for the first Tour de France in 1903 - 5,000 francs, 10,000 francs or 20,000 francs?

263. What colour of Jersey was given to the rider who finished last in the first ever Tour de France - Blue, Grey or Red?

264. Where did the first ever Stage of the Tour de France end - Lyon, Paris or Roubais?

265. Henri Cornet is the youngest ever winner of Le Tour. How old was he when he won it?

266. What "difficult type" of Stage was introduced to Le Tour for the first time in 1905?

267. In 1906 the Red Flag was introduced for each Stage. What did this signify?

268. What, for the first time, was affixed to each rider's bike in the 1914 Tour de France?

269. What similarity did the awarding of a Yellow Jersey to the race leader have with the magazine that sponsored the Tour de France during its early years?

270. What was given to the leading rider in the first ever Tour de France to signify that he led the race - an armband, a bell or a cap?

2004 - LE TOUR - 2

271. How many Stages did Lance Armstrong win on his way to winning the 2004 Tour de France?

272. In what Belgian city did the 2004 Tour de France start - Antwerp, Brussels or Liege?

273. Can you recall the Australian rider who won the Green Jersey?

274. Who won the Final Stage of the 2004 Tour de France - Tom Boonen, Danilo Hondo or Jean-Patrick Nazon?

275. How many Time Trials were there?

276. To the nearest 50,000 euros, how much prize money did Lance Armstrong receive for winning the 2004 Tour de France?

277. Can you name the German rider who was Runner-Up?

278. To the nearest 10, how many riders started the Final Day's Stage?

279. How many Mountain Stages were there in the 2004 Tour de France?

280. Can you name the American actor who was a guest on the podium when the first 3 riders in Le Tour were being presented with their trophies in Paris?

KNOW YOUR NATIONALITY - 2

ALL YOU HAVE TO DO HERE IS ASSOCIATE THE RIDER WITH HIS NATIONALITY

281.	Richard Virenque	German
282.	Abraham Olano	Belgian
283.	Laurent Jalabert	American
284.	Marco Pantani	Spanish
285.	Jan Ullrich	French
286.	Lance Armstrong	Swiss
287.	Robbie McEwen	French
288.	Alex Zulle	Italian
289.	Eddy Merckx	Spanish
290.	Miguel Indurain	Australian

1970s TOUR WINNERS

*ALL YOU HAVE TO DO HERE IS ASSOCIATE THE
RIDER WITH THE YEAR HE WON LE TOUR*

291.	Eddy Merckx	1973
292.	Bernard Hinault	1970
293.	Luis Ocaña	1976
294.	Bernard Thevenet	1972
295.	Eddy Merckx	1978
296.	Lucien Van Impe	1971
297.	Eddy Merckx	1975
298.	Bernard Hinault	1974
299.	Eddy Merckx	1977
300.	Bernard Thevenet	1979

COMBATIVITY WINNERS - 1

ALL YOU HAVE TO DO HERE IS ASSOCIATE THE RIDER WITH THE YEAR HE WON LE TOUR'S COMBATIVITY AWARD

301.	Laurent Jalabert (France)	1986
302.	Massimo Ghirotto (Italy)	2004
303.	Bernard Hinault (France)	1995
304.	Richard Virenque (France)	1988
305.	Claudio Chiappucci (Italy)	1989
306.	Jérôme Simon (France)	2001
307.	Alexandre Vinokourov (Kaz)	1992
308.	Jacky Durand (France)	2003
309.	Hernán Buenahora (Colombia)	1999
310.	Laurent Fignon (France)	1993

LAURENT JALABERT

311. What nationality is Laurent?

312. What colour of overall classification Jersey was the first that Laurent won in Le Tour?

313. What is the highest final position that Laurent has achieved in the Tour de France - 4th, 5th or 6th?

314. In what year did he reach the position in Q313 - 1993, 1994 or 1995?

315. In how many Tours did Laurent actually wear the Yellow Jersey?

316. Name any year in which Laurent wore the Yellow Jersey during a Tour de France.

317. How many times has Laurent won the overall "King of the Mountains" Jersey title in the Tour de France?

318. Can you recall either of the 2 years in which Laurent claimed the overall Green Jersey title?

319. How many times did Laurent win a Stage in the Tour de France?

320. Up to and including 2004, Laurent participated in 10 Tour de France. How many times was he not ranked in the final standings - 3, 4 or 5?

MOST TOURS PARTICIPATED IN

*ALL YOU HAVE TO DO HERE IS ASSOCIATE THE RIDER
WITH THE NUMBER OF TOURS HE STARTED*

321.	Raymond Poulidor (France)	13
322.	Guy Nulens (Belgium)	14
323.	Joop Zoetemelk (Netherlands)	14
324.	André Darrigade (France)	13
325.	Joaquim Agostinho (Portugal)	14
326.	Sean Kelly (Ireland)	15
327.	Lucien Van Impe (Belgium)	14
328.	Jules Deloffre (France)	16
329.	Phil Anderson (Australia)	14
330.	Viatcheslav Ekimov (Russia)	15

LE TOUR - 2

331.   Can you recall the name of the Italian rider who was Runner-Up in the 1991 Tour de France?

332.   In what country did the 1996 Tour de France start?

333.   What colour of Jersey is awarded to the Best Finisher (overall points score) in Le Tour?

334.   Who was Runner-Up in the 1984 Tour de France but came back the next year and won it?

335.   Who was the first American winner of Le Tour?

336.   Can you recall the Swiss rider who was Runner-Up in the 1995 Tour de France?

337.   What British bicycle manufacturer sponsored the winning rider in the 1980 Tour de France?

338.   Who brought Miguel Indurain's winning run to an end in the 1996 Tour de France - Marco Pantani, Bjarne Riis or Jan Ullrich?

339.   Who was the first Irish rider to win the Tour de France?

340.   How many Tours during the 1980s were won by a French rider - 5, 7 or 9?

1999 TOUR DE FRANCE

341. Who won Le Tour?

342. Who was Runner-Up - Jan Ullrich, Richard Virenque or Alex Zulle?

343. What rider won the Green Jersey for the 4th time in his career?

344. Name the rider who won his 5th "King of the Mountains" title.

345. What French "Benoît" was awarded the White Jersey for being the Best Young Rider in Le Tour?

346. Can you recall the name of the Italian rider who captured 4 consecutive Stages?

347. Name the Estonian rider to whom Lance Armstrong lost the Yellow Jersey after Stage 2.

348. This American rider's Tour de France ended after he crashed during Stage 8. Name him.

349. Italy's Giuseppe Guerini won Stage 10 on the second day in the Alps, but how did he manage to fall off his bike less than 1 kilometre from the finishing line?

350. Can you name the Spanish rider who won Stage 12?

TEAM TIME TRIAL WINNERS - 2

ALL YOU HAVE TO DO HERE IS ASSOCIATE THE TEAM WITH
THE YEAR THEY WON THE TEAM TIME TRIAL IN LE TOUR

351.	2001	La Vie Claire (France)
352.	1983	ONCE (Spain)
353.	1989	Crédit Agricole (France)
354.	2004	Panasonic (Netherlands)
355.	1994	Raleigh (Netherlands)
356.	1992	Carrera (Italy)
357.	1981	Super 'U' (France)
358.	2000	GB-MG (Italy)
359.	1985	Coöp-Mercier (France)
360.	1987	US Postal Service (USA)

WHAT TEAM DID I RIDE FOR?

ALL YOU HAVE TO DO HERE IS ASSOCIATE THE RIDER WITH
THE TEAM HE RODE FOR DURING THE 2004 TOUR DE FRANCE

361.	Lance Armstrong	T-Mobile
362.	Jan Ullrich	Quick Step
363.	Iban Mayo	AG2R
364.	Francisco Mancebo	Lotto/Domo
365.	Thor Hushovd	Cofidis
366.	Jean-Patrick Nazon	Illes Balears.com
367.	Stuart O'Grady	CSC World Online
368.	Robbie McEwen	Euskaltel/Euskadi
369.	Ivan Basso	US Postal
370.	Richard Virenque	Crédit Agricole

WHITE JERSEY WINNERS - 1

ALL YOU HAVE TO DO HERE IS ASSOCIATE THE RIDER
WITH THE YEAR HE WON THE BEST YOUNG RIDER

371.	Marco Pantani	1997
372.	Ivan Basso	1991
373.	Erik Breukink	2001
374.	Oscar Sevilla	1994
375.	Raúl Alcala	1976
376.	Vladimir Karpets	1988
377.	Alvaro Mejía	1987
378.	Jan Ullrich	1992
379.	Enrique Martínez Heredia	2002
380.	Eddy Bouwmans	2004

THE GREEN JERSEY

381. According to Le Tour organisers, is green the colour of chance, hope or victory?

382. In what year was the Green Jersey first introduced - 1923, 1933 or 1953?

383. What type of shop was the first sponsor of the Green Jersey?

384. 2 Belgian riders have won 3 Green Jersey competitions each. Name either of them.

385. What nationality was the winner of the first ever Green Jersey in Le Tour - Belgian, French or Swiss?

386. What was the name of the Russian rider who won the Green Jersey in 1991, 1993 and 1994?

387. Into how many different "Stage Types" are Stages in Le Tour divided for awarding points in the Green Jersey classification?

388. Name any 2 of the different Stage Types referred to in Q387.

389. Name the German rider who holds the record for having won the most Green Jerseys with 6 consecutive victories in the competition to his name.

390. Can you name the Irish rider who won 4 Green Jersey competitions?

MIGUEL INDURAIN

391. In how many Tour de France did Miguel participate - 8, 10 or 12?

392. In what year did Miguel participate in his first Tour de France?

393. On how many occasions was Miguel not ranked in the overall positions at the end of a Tour de France?

394. How many times did Miguel win Le Tour?

395. Name any 2 of the years in which Miguel won the overall Yellow Jersey in Le Tour.

396. How many times did Miguel win a Stage in the Tour de France?

397. In what year did Miguel win his first Stage in Le Tour?

398. Can you name any 2 of the riders that finished Runner-Up to Miguel in a Tour de France?

399. For what Team did Miguel ride in all his Tour de France victories?

400. Name either of the 2 riders who won Le Tour immediately prior to Miguel's first victory or immediately after his last victory.

RUNNER-UP AND WINNER
IN CONSECUTIVE YEARS

*ALL YOU HAVE TO DO HERE IS ASSOCIATE THE RIDER WITH
THE YEAR HE FINISHED RUNNER-UP AND WINNER IN
CONSECUTIVE YEARS IN LE TOUR (one rider 2 years apart)*

401.	Nicolas Frantz	1987 & 1988
402.	Bernard Hinault	1925 & 1926
403.	François Faber	1966 & 1968
404.	Ottavio Bottecchia	1984 & 1985
405.	Pedro Delgado	1926 & 1927
406.	Joop Zoetemelk	1996 & 1997
407.	Lucien Buysse	1985 & 1986
408.	Greg Lemond	1979 & 1980
409.	Jan Ullrich	1923 & 1924
410.	Jan Janssen	1908 & 1909

2004 STAGE WINNERS

ALL YOU HAVE TO DO HERE IS ASSOCIATE THE RIDER
WITH THE STAGE HE WON

411.	Prologue	Thor Hushovd
412.	Stage 1	Juan Miguel Mercado
413.	Stage 5	Lance Armstrong
414.	Stage 7	Ivan Basso
415.	Stage 8	Aitor Gonzalez
416.	Stage 11	Fabian Cancellara
417.	Stage 12	Stuart O'Grady
418.	Stage 14	David Moncoutié
419.	Stage 16	Jann Kirsipuu
420.	Stage 18	Filippo Pozzato

THE POLKA-DOT JERSEY

421. What rider is presented with the Polka-Dot Jersey in Le Tour?

422. In what year was the "King of the Mountains" classification first calculated in Le Tour - 1931, 1932 or 1933?

423. What nationality was the rider who was the first to win the "King of the Mountains" - French, Italian or Spanish?

424. In what year was the Polka-Dot Jersey first given to a rider to wear in Le Tour - 1974, 1975 or 1976?

425. What company was the first to sponsor the "King of the Mountains" Polka-Dot Jersey - Aquarel, Citroen or Poulain?

426. Why was the Jersey a red and white Polka-Dot Jersey?

427. Can you name the French rider who has won the most "King of the Mountains" titles?

428. What nationality was the first rider, and future winner of Le Tour, to wear the Polka-Dot Jersey - Colombian, Dutch or Italian?

429. In what 2 mountain ranges must a rider excel to be crowned "King of the Mountains"?

430. Can you name the Colombian rider who won the "King of the Mountains" title in 1985 and 1987?

KNOW YOUR NATIONALITY - 3

ALL YOU HAVE TO DO HERE IS ASSOCIATE THE RIDER WITH HIS NATIONALITY

431.	Steve Bauer	Colombian
432.	Joseba Beloki	American
433.	Viatcheslav Ekimov	German
434.	George Hincapie	French
435.	Erik Zabel	Spanish
436.	Santiago Botero	Irish
437.	Bernard Hinault	American
438.	Sean Kelly	Spanish
439.	Roberto Heras	Canadian
440.	Tyler Hamilton	Russian

JAN ULLRICH

441.   What nationality is Jan?

442.   In how many Tours de France has Jan participated - 7, 8 or 9?

443.   In what year during the 1990s did Jan participate in his first Tour de France?

444.   On how many occasions has Jan not been ranked in the overall positions at the end of a Tour de France?

445.   In what year did Jan win his only Tour de France?

446.   Name the French rider who finished Runner-Up to Jan in Q445.

447.   How many times has Jan won a Stage in the Tour de France - 6, 7 or 8?

448.   In what year did Jan claim his first Stage victory - 1996, 1997 or 1998?

449.   For what German Team did Jan ride when he won the Tour de France?

450.   How many times has Jan finished in Le Tour's Final Top 5 positions?

2000 TOP 10 FINISHERS

ALL YOU HAVE TO DO HERE IS ASSOCIATE THE RIDER WITH HIS PLACING IN THE 2000 TOUR DE FRANCE

451.	Daniele Nardello (Italy), Mapei-Quick Step	2
452.	Fernando Escartin (Spain), Kelme-Costa Blanca	10
453.	Francisco Mancebo (Spain), Banesto	5
454.	Richard Virenque (France), Team Polti	9
455.	Christophe Moreau (France), Festina	1
456.	Joseba Beloki (Spain), Festina	8
457.	Lance Armstrong (USA), US Postal Service	4
458.	Jan Ullrich (Germany), Team Deutsche Telekom	6
459.	Santiago Botero (Colombia), Kelme-Costa Blanca	3
460.	Roberto Heras (Spain), Kelme-Costa Blanca	7

1980s TOUR WINNERS

ALL YOU HAVE TO DO HERE IS ASSOCIATE THE RIDER
WITH THE YEAR HE WON LE TOUR

461.	Pedro Delgado	1986
462.	Bernard Hinault	1980
463.	Greg Lemond	1982
464.	Laurent Fignon	1985
465.	Bernard Hinault	1987
466.	Joop Zoetemelk	1989
467.	Greg Lemond	1988
468.	Bernard Hinault	1983
469.	Stephen Roche	1984
470.	Laurent Fignon	1981

SEAN KELLY

471. What nationality is Sean?

472. What is the highest final position that Sean has achieved in the Tour de France - 2nd, 3rd or 4th?

473. In what year did he reach the position in Q472 - 1983, 1984 or 1985?

474. In how many Tour de France did Sean actually wear the Yellow Jersey?

475. How many times did Sean win the overall Green Jersey title in the Tour de France?

476. Can you recall any 2 of the years in which Sean claimed the Green Jersey title?

477. How many times did Sean win a Stage in the Tour de France?

478. Sean participated in 14 Tour de France. How many times was he not ranked in the final standings - 0, 1 or 2?

479. In what year during the 1970s did he claim his first Stage victory?

480. In what year during the 1980s did he claim his last Stage victory in the Tour de France?

KING OF THE MOUNTAINS

481. This French rider won 4 consecutive Polka-Dot Jerseys between 1994 and 1997. Can you name him?

482. This famous rider not only won the "King of the Mountains" in 1969 and 1970, but he also won Le Tour. What is his name?

483. Apart from being the first Italian winner of the "King of the Mountains" title, what other "first" can Gino Bartali claim in relation to the "King of the Mountains" title?

484. Who in 1934 became the first French rider to win the "King of the Mountains" title - Louison Bobet, Raphael Geminiani or René Vietto?

485. Can you recall the name of the Spanish rider who won 6 Polka-Dot Jerseys between 1954 and 1964?

486. Name the Swiss rider who won the 1993 "King of the Mountains" title.

487. Apart from Eddy Merckx, can you name the other Belgian rider who has won 8 Mountain Stages in Le Tour?

488. This Scotsman won the "King of the Mountains" title in 1984. Who is he?

489. Name the Italian rider who was crowned "King of the Mountains" in 1991 and 1992.

490. This Dutch rider won the Polka-Dot Jersey in 1988 and was Runner-Up to Pedro Delgado in Le Tour the same year. Who is he?

LE TOUR STAGE FINISHES

ALL YOU HAVE TO DO HERE IS ASSOCIATE THE CITY WITH THE NUMBER OF TIMES LE TOUR HAS HOSTED A STAGE FINISH THERE

491.	Nantes	33
492.	Briançon	45
493.	Metz	32
494.	Bordeaux	30
495.	Marseille	78
496.	Pau	30
497.	Caen	96
498.	Paris	37
499.	Bayonne	54
500.	Bagnères-de-Luchon	28

PEDRO DELGADO

501.   What nationality is Pedro?

502.   In how many Tour de France did Pedro participate - 10, 11 or 12?

503.   In what year did Pedro participate in his first Tour de France?

504.   On how many occasions was Pedro not ranked in the overall positions at the end of a Tour de France?

505.   In what year did Pedro win his only Tour de France?

506.   Who finished Runner-Up to Pedro in Q505?

507.   How many times did Pedro win a Stage in the Tour de France - 4, 6 or 8?

508.   In what year did Pedro claim his first Stage victory - 1984, 1985 or 1986?

509.   For what Team did Pedro ride when he won the Tour de France?

510.   How many times did Pedro finish Runner-Up in Le Tour?

2000 TOUR DE FRANCE

511. Who won Le Tour?

512. How many consecutive overall Yellow Jerseys had the rider in Q511 won after winning this Tour de France?

513. What rider won the Green Jersey?

514. Name the Colombian rider who won the "King of the Mountains".

515. What Spanish "Francisco" was awarded the White Jersey for being the Best Young Rider in Le Tour?

516. Can you recall the British rider who captured Stage 1?

517. Name the Belgian rider who won Stages 2 and 3.

518. What Team won the Stage 4 Team Time Trial - ONCE, Telekom or US Postal?

519. After what Stage did Lance Armstrong lead the General Classification for the first time in Le Tour - 2, 6 or 10?

520. Can you name the German rider who won the Final Stage - Stage 21: Paris Eiffel Tower to Champs- Elysées?

THE NEARLY MEN 1995-2004

*ALL YOU HAVE TO DO HERE IS ASSOCIATE THE RIDER
WITH THE YEAR HE FINISHED RUNNER-UP IN LE TOUR*

521.	1995	Jan Ullrich
522.	1996	Joseba Beloki
523.	1997	Jan Ullrich
524.	1998	Richard Virenque
525.	1999	Jan Ullrich
526.	2000	Alex Zulle
527.	2001	Andreas Kloden
528.	2002	Jan Ullrich
529.	2003	Alex Zulle
530.	2004	Jan Ullrich

2004 TEAM MANAGERS

ALL YOU HAVE TO HERE IS ASSOCIATE THE MANAGER
WITH THE TEAM HE MANAGED

531.	Johan Bruyneel	Rabobank
532.	Roger Legeay	Quick Step
533.	Marc Sergeant	T-Mobile
534.	Walter Godefroot	Cofidis
535.	Theo de Rooy	US Postal
536.	Miguel Madariaga	CSC
537.	Cyrille Guimard	Lotto-Domo
538.	Alvaro Crespi	Illes Balears-Banesto
539.	José-Miguel Echavarri	Crédit Agricole
540.	Bjarne Riis	Euskaltel-Euskadi

BJARNE RIIS

541.   What nationality is Bjarne?

542.   In how many Tour de France did Bjarne participate - 7, 8 or 9?

543.   In what year during the 1980s did Bjarne participate in his first
        Tour de France?

544.   On how many occasions was Bjarne not ranked in the overall
        positions at the end of a Tour de France?

545.   In what year did Bjarne win his only Tour de France?

546.   Name the German rider who finished Runner-Up to Bjarne in
        Q545.

547.   How many times did Bjarne win a Stage in the Tour de France -
        4, 6 or 8?

548.   In what year did Bjarne claim his first Stage victory - 1992, 1993
        or 1994?

549.   For what German Team did Bjarne ride when he won the Tour de
        France?

550.   How many times did Bjarne finish in Le Tour's Final Top 5
        positions?

2004 - LE TOUR - 3

551. A rider who finished in the Top 5 places of Le Tour also finished in Runner-Up place in the "King of the Mountains" competition. Name the rider.

552. Who won the White Jersey for Best Young Rider - Sandy Casar, Vladimir Karpets or Thomas Voeckler?

553. For what Team did the rider in Q552 ride - Brioches La Boulangère, FDJ or Illes Balears?

554. A 2004 Yellow Jersey winner entered the Tour as the French National Champion. Can you name him?

555. Name the former Green Jersey winner who finished in 3rd place in this year's race for the Green Jersey.

556. What Team won the overall General Classification title - CSC, T-Mobile or US Postal?

557. How many points are awarded to the winner of a Mountain Stage - 30, 35 or 40?

558. For what "Quick" Team did the "King of the Mountains", Richard Virenque, ride?

559. What "Channel" did the US Postal Team announce would be their main sponsor for the 2005 Tour de France?

560. In what position did Jan Ullrich finish in Le Tour?

LUCIEN AIMAR

561.   What nationality is Lucien?

562.   How many times did Lucien win Le Tour?

563.   In how many Tour de France did Lucien participate - 9, 10 or
        11?

564.   In what year did Lucien participate in his first Tour de France -
        1964, 1965 or 1966?

565.   On how many occasions was Lucien not ranked in the overall
        positions at the end of a Tour de France?

566.   What future Dutch winner of Le Tour finished Runner-Up to
        Lucien when Lucien won the 1966 Tour de France?

567.   How many times did Lucien win a Stage in the Tour de France -
        1, 3 or 5?

568.   For what American car manufacture-sponsored Team did Lucien
        ride when he won Le Tour?

569.   How many times has Lucien finished in the Top 10 of Le Tour -
        3, 4 or 5?

570.   On how many occasions did Lucien finish as Runner-Up in Le
        Tour?

SPANISH RIDERS

571.   Can you recall the Spanish rider who won a Stage in the Tour de France in 1985, 1986, 1987 and 1990 - Eduardo Chozas, Manuel Galera or Javier Luquin?

572.   Can you name the Spanish rider who won Stage 1 of the 1976 Tour de France - Ventura Diaz, José-Luis Viejo or Juan Zarano?

573.   Name the Spanish rider who finished Runner-Up in the 2002 Tour de France and finished in 3rd place in both the 2000 and 2001 Tour de France.

574.   This rider, with a Californian city as a surname, took part in 3 Tour de France (1997-1999) with a highest overall final placing of 55th. Name him.

575.   Can you name the rider who finished 2nd in 1987, 1st in 1988 and 3rd in 1989?

576.   What Spanish rider has won Le Tour the most times?

577.   Can you name the Spanish rider who won Stage 2 of the 1992 Tour de France - Javier Murguialday, Miguel Pacheco or Vittorio Ruiz?

578.   How many times did David Etxebarria win a Stage in the 1999 Tour de France - 2, 3 or 4?

579.   Who, with the initials F.E., took part in 9 Tour de France between 1986 and 1994, achieving a highest overall position of 12th in 1987 when he also won a Stage?

580. Sharing the same surname as a famous Spanish golfer, this rider won the "King of the Mountains" Jersey in 3 consecutive years from 1965 to 1967 (finishing in 2nd place overall in 1967). Name him.

KNOW YOUR NATIONALITY - 4

*ALL YOU HAVE TO DO HERE IS ASSOCIATE THE RIDER
WITH HIS NATIONALITY*

581.	Richard Virenque	Italian
582.	Bobby Julich	French
583.	Joseba Beloki	Italian
584.	Jacky Durand	Spanish
585.	Mario Cipollini	Colombian
586.	Pedro Delgado	Dutch
587.	Baden Cooke	Spanish
588.	Ivan Basso	Australian
589.	Santiago Botero	American
590.	Erik Dekker	French

JOOP ZOETEMELK

591.   What nationality is Joop?

592.   In how many Tour de France did Joop participate - 15, 16 or
       17?

593.   In what year during the 1970s did Joop participate in his first
       Tour de France?

594.   On how many occasions was Joop not ranked in the overall
       positions at the end of a Tour de France?

595.   In what year did Joop win his only Tour de France?

596.   Can you recall the name of the Dutch rider who finished
       Runner-Up to Joop in Q595?

597.   How many times did Joop win a Stage in the Tour de France - 9,
       10 or 11?

598.   In what year did Joop claim his first Stage victory - 1973, 1974
       or 1975?

599.   For what British Team did Joop ride when he won the Tour de
       France?

600.   How many times did Joop finish in Le Tour's Final Top 5
       positions - 3, 5 or 11?

LE TOUR INCIDENTS

ALL YOU HAVE TO DO HERE IS ASSOCIATE THE INCIDENT WITH THE YEAR IT HAPPENED IN LE TOUR

601. Tom Simpson dies during the climb of Mont Ventoux. 1910

602. Adolphe Helière dives into the sea on a rest day and drowns. 1978

603. Tour photographers go on strike. 1998

604. Fans protest by throwing nails in the streets. 1987

605. Fabio Casartelli falls off his bike descending the Portet d'Aspet and hits his head on a stone. He is taken to hospital and dies there. 1968

606. Francisco Cepeda dies after breaking his skull after falling off his bike. 1967

607. Riders protest over early start times in Le Tour. 1935

608. Riders object angrily to Le Tour's first doping tests. 1905

609. Riders react angrily to police raids and the treatment by the police of members of the TVM Team. 1966

610. Journalists block the road during Le Tour. 1985

SPONSORS 2004 TOUR

611. What car manufacturer sponsored the White Jersey in Le Tour?

612. Can you name any 2 of the 4 companies that were accredited with official Tour de France "Club Membership" for the 2004 Tour?

613. What sportswear company manufactured the 4 principal Jerseys for the 2004 Tour?

614. Name the Japanese motorcycle manufacturer that was a principal supplier in Le Tour.

615. What company (3 letters) sponsored the Green Jersey?

616. Can you name the tyre manufacturer that was a principal supplier in Le Tour?

617. What company, along with US Postal, was the principal sponsor to Lance Armstrong's Team?

618. What company sponsored the "King of the Mountains" competition?

619. What company sponsored the Yellow Jersey?

620. What Paris-based "resort" was the Cadets Juniors Partner?

THE TOP 10 OF 2004 - 1

THE FOLLOWING RIDERS MADE UP THE TOP 10 PLACES. ALL YOU HAVE TO DO IS ASSOCIATE THEM WITH THEIR FINAL POSITION

621.	Carlos Sastre	4
622.	José Azevedo	3
623.	Andreas Kloden	8
624.	Lance Armstrong	6
625.	Georg Totschnig	2
626.	Ivan Basso	9
627.	Levi Leipheimer	5
628.	Francisco Mancebo	10
629.	Oscar Pereiro	7
630.	Jan Ullrich	1

BEST SPRINTER WINNERS - 2

*ALL YOU HAVE TO DO HERE IS ASSOCIATE THE RIDER
WITH THE YEAR HE WON THE GREEN JERSEY*

631.	Rik Van Linden	1992
632.	Djamolidin Abdoujaparov	1987
633.	Jacques Esclassan	1982
634.	Eddy Merckx	1994
635.	Jean-Paul Van Poppel	2000
636.	Laurent Jalabert	1977
637.	Erik Zabel	1981
638.	Freddy Maertens	2002
639.	Robbie McEwen	1971
640.	Sean Kelly	1975

2001 TOUR DE FRANCE

641. Who won Le Tour?

642. Can you name the Spanish rider who finished in 3rd place?

643. What German rider won the Green Jersey?

644. Name the French rider who won the "King of the Mountains".

645. Can you name the Dutch "Erik" who won Stage 8: Colmar to Pontarlier?

646. What Spanish "Oscar" was awarded the White Jersey for being the Best Young Rider in Le Tour?

647. Who was the highest-placed French rider, finishing Le Tour in 6th position?

648. What Team won the Stage 5 Team Time Trial - Crédit Agricole, Festina or ONCE?

649. Can you name the Estonian rider who won Stage 6: Commercy to Strasbourg?

650. Name either of the 2 Kelme riders who finished in the Top 10.

LUCIEN VAN IMPE

651. What nationality is Lucien?

652. How many times did Lucien win Le Tour?

653. In how many Tour de France did Lucien participate - 15, 16 or 17?

654. In what year did Lucien participate in his first Tour de France - 1969, 1970 or 1971?

655. On how many occasions was Lucien not ranked in the overall positions at the end of a Tour de France?

656. What future Dutch winner of Le Tour finished Runner-Up to Lucien when Lucien won the 1976 Tour de France?

657. How many times did Lucien win a Stage in the Tour de France - 9, 10 or 11?

658. Apart from the Yellow Jersey, what other overall classification Jersey did Lucien win in Le Tour?

659. How many times did Lucien win the Jersey in Q658?

660. On how many occasions did Lucien finish as Runner-Up in Le Tour?

COMBATIVITY WINNERS - 2

*ALL YOU HAVE TO DO HERE IS ASSOCIATE THE RIDER WITH
THE YEAR HE WON LE TOUR'S COMBATIVITY AWARD*

661.	Bernard Hinault (France)	2002
662.	Erik Dekker (Netherlands)	1994
663.	Richard Virenque (France)	1990
664.	Eduardo Chozas (Spain)	1984
665.	Jacky Durand (France)	1987
666.	Claudio Chiappucci (Italy)	2000
667.	Eros Poli (Italy)	1985
668.	Maarten Ducrot (Netherlands)	1991
669.	Laurent Jalabert (France)	1997
670.	Pedro Delgado (Spain)	1998

LE TOUR - 3

671. Apart from French, can you name the nationalities of any other 2 Tour de France winners during the 1980s?

672. Who finished Runner-Up to Laurent Fignon in the 1984 Tour de France - Pedro Delgado, Bernard Hinault or Greg Lemond?

673. Can you name the French car manufacturer that sponsored the winner of the Tour de France in 4 consecutive years from 1981 to 1984?

674. What year's Tour de France is the fastest in the history of the competition - 1983, 1993 or 2003?

675. Who was the last Dutch rider to win Le Tour?

676. To the nearest 1 minute, by what margin did Lance Armstrong win the 2004 Tour de France?

677. Can you recall the name of the German rider who was Runner-Up in the 2004 Tour de France?

678. Name any 3 of the 5 riders who have won 5 or more Tour de France.

679. Name the "Strongman" Quick Step rider who finished the Tour in 15th place.

680. What Scandinavian rider won the 1996 Tour de France?

WHITE JERSEY WINNERS - 2

ALL YOU HAVE TO DO HERE IS ASSOCIATE THE RIDER
WITH THE YEAR HE WON THE BEST YOUNG RIDER TITLE

681.	Jan Ullrich	1977
682.	Jean-René Bernaudeau	1986
683.	Denis Menchov	1996
684.	Fabio Parra	1989
685.	Gilles Delion	1995
686.	Dietrich Thurau	1990
687.	Marco Pantani	1979
688.	Fabrice Philipot	2000
689.	Francisco Mancebo	1985
690.	Andrew Hampsten	2003

MARCO PANTANI

691.   What nationality is Marco?

692.   In how many Tour de France did Marco participate - 5, 6 or 7?

693.   In what year during the 1990s did Marco participate in his first Tour de France?

694.   On how many occasions was Marco not ranked in the overall positions at the end of a Tour de France?

695.   In what year did Marco win his only Tour de France?

696.   Name the German rider who finished Runner-Up to Marco in Q695.

697.   How many times did Marco win a Stage in the Tour de France - 6, 7 or 8?

698.   In what year did Marco claim his first Stage victory - 1993, 1994 or 1995?

699.   For what Italian Team did Marco ride when he won the Tour de France?

700.   How many times did Marco finish in Le Tour's Final Top 5 positions?

KING OF THE MOUNTAIN WINNERS - 2

ALL YOU HAVE TO DO HERE IS ASSOCIATE THE RIDER WITH THE YEAR HE WON THE POLKA-DOT JERSEY

701.	Domingo Perurena	1999
702.	Santiago Botero	1978
703.	Stephen Rooks	1971
704.	Mariano Martinez	1987
705.	Robert Millar	2000
706.	Claudio Chiappucci	1976
707.	Giancarlo Bellini	1988
708.	Richard Virenque	1974
709.	Lucien Van Impe	1984
710.	Luis Herrera	1992

THE TOP 10 OF 2004 - 2

THE FOLLOWING RIDERS MADE UP THE TOP 10 PLACES.
ALL YOU HAVE TO DO IS ASSOCIATE THEM WITH THEIR TEAM

711.	Carlos Sastre	Gerolsteiner
712.	José Azevedo	Phonak
713.	Andreas Kloden	US Postal
714.	Lance Armstrong	CSC
715.	Georg Totschnig	T-Mobile
716.	Ivan Basso	Illes Balears
717.	Levi Leipheimer	US Postal
718.	Francisco Mancebo	T-Mobile
719.	Oscar Pereiro	Rabobank
720.	Jan Ullrich	CSC

JAN JANSSEN

721. What nationality is Jan?

722. In how many Tour de France did Jan participate - 7, 8 or 9?

723. In what year during the 1960s did Jan participate in his first Tour de France?

724. On how many occasions was Jan not ranked in the overall positions at the end of a Tour de France?

725. In what year did Jan win his only Tour de France - 1968, 1969 or 1970?

726. Apart from the Yellow Jersey, what other overall classification Jersey did Jan win in the Tour de France?

727. How many times did Jan win the Jersey in Q726?

728. How many Stages did Jan win in Le Tour - 3, 5 or 7?

729. What was the most number of Stages that Jan won in a single Tour de France - 2, 3 or 4?

730. How many times did Jan finish in Le Tour's Final Top 5 positions - 1, 2 or 3?

MOST YELLOW JERSEYS IN LE TOUR

ALL YOU HAVE TO DO HERE IS ASSOCIATE THE RIDER WITH THE NUMBER OF YELLOW JERSEYS HE WON IN LE TOUR

731.	Miguel Indurain (Spain)	34
732.	André Leducq (France)	66
733.	Jacques Anquetil (France)	39
734.	Ottavio Bottecchia (Italy)	96
735.	Antonin Magne (France)	35
736.	Eddy Merckx (Belgium)	60
737.	Nicolas Frantz (Luxembourg)	79
738.	Louison Bobet (France)	51
739.	Bernard Hinault (France)	37
740.	Lance Armstrong (USA)	33

RICHARD VIRENQUE

741.   What nationality is Richard?

742.   What was the highest final position that Richard achieved in the Tour de France?

743.   In what year did he reach the position in Q742 - 1997, 1998 or 1999?

744.   In how many Tour de France did Richard actually wear the Yellow Jersey?

745.   Name any year in which Richard wore the Yellow Jersey during a Tour de France.

746.   How many times did Richard win the "King of the Mountains" title in the Tour de France?

747.   Can you recall any 2 of the years in which Richard claimed the "King of the Mountains" title?

748.   How many times did Richard win a Stage in the Tour de France?

749.   Richard participated in 12 Tour de France. How many times was he not ranked in the final standings - 1, 3 or 5?

750.   In what year did he claim his first Stage victory?

FRENCH WINNERS OF LE TOUR

751.   Up to and including the 2004 Tour de France, how many different French riders have won the race - 21, 31 or 41?

752.   How many French riders have won Le Tour on more than 1 occasion?

753.   Who was the last French winner of Le Tour to finish Runner-Up in Le Tour?

754.   In what year did the rider in Q753 finish Runner-Up - 1989, 1990 or 1991?

755.   How many French victories have there been in the history of Le Tour (up to 2004) - 36, 46 or 56?

756.   Who was the last French rider to win Le Tour?

757.   In what year did the rider in Q756 win the Yellow Jersey?

758.   How many French riders have won more than 2 Tour de France?

759.   Name any 2 of the French riders that have won more than 2 Tour de France.

760.   Can you name the French rider who won Le Tour in 1983 and then successfully defended the Yellow Jersey the following year?

TOUR WINNERS - 2

*ALL YOU HAVE TO DO HERE IS ASSOCIATE THE RIDER
WITH THE YEAR HE WON LE TOUR*

761.	Marco Pantani	1980
762.	Joop Zoetemelk	1993
763.	Lance Armstrong	1986
764.	Bernard Hinault	1984
765.	Eddy Merckx	1999
766.	Pedro Delgado	1972
767.	Greg Lemond	1997
768.	Lauren Fignon	1998
769.	Miguel Indurain	1982
770.	Jan Ullrich	1988

2002 TOUR DE FRANCE

771. Who won Le Tour?

772. Can you name the Colombian rider who finished in 4th place?

773. What Australian rider won the Green Jersey?

774. Name the French rider who won the "King of the Mountains".

775. What Italian rider was awarded the White Jersey for being the Best Young Rider in Le Tour?

776. Name the Spanish rider who finished second to Lance Armstrong in Stage 11: Pau to La Mongie.

777. What "David" was the highest-placed French rider, finishing Le Tour in 13th position?

778. What Team won the Stage 5 Team Time Trial - Cofidis, ONCE or US Postal?

779. Name any 1 of the 3 ONCE riders who finished in the Top 10.

780. Can you name the 2002 rider, whose father was a multiple Tour de France winner, who finished 3rd in Stage 15: Vaison-la-Romaine to Les Deux-Alpes?

LAURENT FIGNON

781. How many times did Laurent win Le Tour?

782. Name any year in which Laurent won the overall Yellow Jersey.

783. In how many Tour de France did Laurent participate - 10, 11 or 12?

784. In what year did Laurent participate in his first Tour de France?

785. On how many occasions was Laurent not ranked in the overall positions at the end of a Tour de France?

786. What French rider finished Runner-Up to Laurent when he won Le Tour in 1984?

787. How many times did Laurent win a Stage in the Tour de France - 9, 10 or 11?

788. In what year did Laurent claim his first Stage victory - 1983, 1984 or 1985?

789. For what French car manufacturer-sponsored Team did Laurent ride when he won his first Tour de France?

790. How many times did Laurent finish as Runner-Up in Le Tour?

1990 TOUR DE FRANCE

791. Who won Le Tour?

792. Can you name the Italian rider who finished in 2nd place?

793. What German rider won the Green Jersey?

794. Name the French rider who won the "King of the Mountains".

795. Can you name the "Erik" who finished Le Tour in 3rd place?

796. What Team won the "Best Team" prize in Le Tour - Banesto, ONCE or Z?

797. Who was Le Tour's White Jersey winner for being the Best Young Rider - Gilles Delion, Dimitri Konyshev or Pascal Lino?

798. Apart from the rider in Q791, can you name any other rider who wore the Yellow Jersey in Le Tour?

799. Can you name the Spanish rider who was voted Le Tour's most aggressive rider?

800. A future Tour de France winner finished in 4th place in the "King of the Mountains" competition. Name him.

ROBBIE McEWEN

801.   What nationality is Robbie?

802.   What is the highest final position that Robbie has achieved in the Tour de France - 29th, 59th or 89th?

803.   In what year did he reach the position in Q802 - 1997, 1998 or 1999?

804.   In how many Tours has Robbie actually worn the Yellow Jersey?

805.   In what year did Robbie win his first Stage in Le Tour - 1999, 2000 or 2001?

806.   How many times has Robbie won the overall Green Jersey title in the Tour de France?

807.   Can you recall the first year in which Robbie claimed the Green Jersey title?

808.   How many times has Robbie won a Stage in the Tour de France?

809.   Robbie has participated in 7 Tour de France. How many times was he not ranked in the final standings - 0, 1 or 2?

810.   Follwing on from Q805, where did this famous Stage end?

SPANISH PODIUM APPEARANCES

*ALL YOU HAVE TO DO HERE IS MATCH THE RIDER WITH
THE YEAR HE APPEARED ON THE PODIUM AND HIS
PLACING IN LE TOUR THAT YEAR*

811.	Miguel Indurain	1973 (1st)
812.	Luis Ocaña	1988 (1st)
813.	Julio Jimenez	1973 (3rd)
814.	Pedro Delgado	1952 (3rd)
815.	Angel Arroyo	1967 (2nd)
816.	Federico Bahamontes	1963 (3rd)
817.	Bernardo Ruiz	1983 (2nd)
818.	Vicente Lopez-Carril	1991 (1st)
819.	José Perez-Frances	1974 (3rd)
820.	José-Manuel Fuente	1959 (1st)

ITALIAN PODIUM APPEARANCES

ALL YOU HAVE TO DO HERE IS MATCH THE RIDER WITH THE YEAR HE APPEARED ON THE PODIUM AND HIS PLACING IN LE TOUR THAT YEAR

821.	Gino Bartali	1965 (3rd)
822.	Marco Pantani	1960 (1st)
823.	Gianni Motta	1990 (2nd)
824.	Franco Balmamion	1961 (2nd)
825.	Claudio Chiappucci	1938 (1st)
826.	Gastone Nencini	1965 (1st)
827.	Guido Carlesi	1949 (1st)
828.	Felice Gimondi	1992 (3rd)
829.	Gianni Bugno	1967 (3rd)
830.	Fausto Coppi	1998 (1st)

FAUSTO COPPI

831.   What nationality is Fausto?

832.   How many times did Fausto win Le Tour?

833.   Name any year in which Fausto won Le Tour.

834.   In how many Tour de France did Fausto participate - 3, 4 or 5?

835.   Can you name the Italian rider, and winner of the Yellow Jersey the previous year, who finished Runner-Up to Fausto when Fausto won his first Tour de France?

836.   Apart from the Yellow Jersey, can you name the other overall classification Jersey that Fausto won in a Tour de France?

837.   How many Stages did Fausto win in total in Le Tour - 7, 8 or 9?

838.   What was the lowest position in which Fausto finished a Tour de France - 2nd, 5th or 10th?

839.   What is the highest number of Stages ever won by Fausto in a single Tour de France?

840.   For what Team did Fausto ride when he won his first Tour de France - Automoto, La Sportive or Team Italy?

ALPE D'HUEZ STAGE WINNERS

ALL YOU HAVE TO DO HERE IS MATCH THE RIDER WITH
THE YEAR HE WON THE STAGE TO ALPE D'HUEZ

841.	Roberto Conti (Italy)	1988
842.	Iban Mayo (Spain)	1992
843.	Bernard Hinault (France)	1991
844.	Andrew Hampsten (USA)	2003
845.	Luis Herrera (Colombia)	1987
846.	Stephen Rooks (Netherlands)	1999
847.	Lance Armstrong (USA)	1986
848.	Giuseppe Guerini (Italy)	1994
849.	Federico Echave (Spain)	2004
850.	Gianni Bugno (Italy)	1984

Photographs © Barry Quick Photography

Photographs © Barry Quick Photography

Photographs © Barry Quick Photography

Photographs © Barry Quick Photography

Photographs © Barry Quick Photography

Photographs © Barry Quick Photography

Photographs © Barry Quick Photography

Photographs © John Miranda

Photographs © Mark Schmisseur

SWISS RIDERS

851.   Who was the first Swiss rider to win the Tour de France - Leo
        Amberg, Ferdi Kubler or Fritz Schär?

852.   In what year did the rider in Q851 win Le Tour - 1948, 1949 or
        1950?

853.   Name the Swiss rider who finished Runner-Up in the 1995 Tour
        de France.

854.   Can you recall the Swiss rider who won 3 Stages in the 1993 Tour
        de France?

855.   What was Urs Zimmermann's highest overall placing in a Tour
        de France?

856.   Hugo Koblet won the 1951 Tour de France. How many Stages
        did he win on his way to victory - 1, 3 or 5?

857.   What was the highest position in which Tony Rominger finished
        a Tour de France?

858.   How many Stages did Leo Amberg win in Le Tour - 2, 3 or 4?

859.   Can you name the Swiss rider who wore the Yellow Jersey in 2
        Tour de France but never won the Jersey overall?

860.   Can you name the Swiss rider who won the "King of the
        Mountains" Jersey in the 1993 Tour de France?

PORTUGUESE RIDERS

861. How many times has a Portuguese rider won Le Tour?

862. Can you name the Portuguese rider who wore the Yellow Jersey in the 1989 Tour de France?

863. Can you recall the Portuguese rider who won 2 Stages in the 1969 Tour de France?

864. What was Antonio Barbosa's highest overall placing in a Tour de France - 5th, 10th or 15th?

865. Can you name the Portuguese rider who won a Stage in the Tour de France in 3 consecutive years during the 1980s?

866. Name the Portuguese rider who won Stage 4 in the 2004 Tour de France.

867. Can you recall the Portuguese rider who won Stage 5 in the 1984 Tour de France - Benediti Ferreira, Fernando Ferreira or Paulo Ferreira?

868. How many Stages did the rider in Q867 win overall in Le Tour?

869. Can you name the Portuguese rider who won a Stage in the 1969, 1973, 1977 and 1979 Tour de France?

870. To the nearest 10 places, what was the highest position in which Acacio Da Silva finished a Tour de France?

COLOMBIAN STAGE WINNERS

*ALL YOU HAVE TO DO HERE IS MATCH THE COLOMBIAN
RIDER WITH THE YEAR HE WON A STAGE IN LE TOUR*

871.	Nelson Rodriguez	1985
872.	Santiago Botero	1993
873.	Oliverio Rincon	2002
874.	Luis Herrera	1996
875.	Fabio Parra	2000
876.	Santiago Botero	1985
877.	Pico Gonzalez	1984
878.	Felix Cardenas	1988
879.	Luis Herrera	1994
880.	Fabio Parra	2001

DUTCH PODIUM APPEARANCES

ALL YOU HAVE TO DO HERE IS MATCH THE RIDER WITH
THE YEAR HE APPEARED ON THE PODIUM AND HIS PLACING
IN LE TOUR THAT YEAR

881.	Erik Breukink	1966 (2nd)
882.	Jan Janssen	1980 (1st)
883.	Hennie Kuiper	1968 (1st)
884.	Steven Rooks	1979 (2nd)
885.	Joop Zoetemelk	1982 (3rd)
886.	Peter Winnen	1977 (2nd)
887.	Jan Janssen	1980 (2nd)
888.	Hennie Kuiper	1983 (3rd)
889.	Johan Van der Velde	1990 (3rd)
890.	Joop Zoetemelk	1988 (2nd)

LUXEMBOURG PODIUM APPEARANCES

*ALL YOU HAVE TO DO HERE IS MATCH THE RIDER WITH
THE YEAR HE APPEARED ON THE PODIUM AND HIS PLACING
IN LE TOUR THAT YEAR*

891.	François Faber	1926 (2nd)
892.	Nicolas Frantz	1910 (2nd)
893.	Charly Gaul	1909 (1st)
894.	François Faber	1928 (1st)
895.	Nicolas Frantz	1955 (3rd)
896.	Charly Gaul	1927 (1st)
897.	François Faber	1958 (1st)
898.	Nicolas Frantz	1908 (2nd)
899.	Charly Gaul	1924 (2nd)
900.	Nicolas Frantz	1961 (3rd)

GERMAN STAGE WINNERS

ALL YOU HAVE TO DO HERE IS MATCH THE GERMAN RIDER WITH THE YEAR HE WON A STAGE IN LE TOUR

901.	Olaf Ludwig	1966
902.	Rolf Golz	1979
903.	Jens Voight	2003
904.	Jens Heppner	1993
905.	Rudi Altig	1998
906.	Jan Ullrich	1970
907.	Dietrich Thurau	2002
908.	Erik Zabel	1988
909.	Rolf Wolfshohl	1978
910.	Klaus-Peter Thaler	2001

ITALIAN YELLOW
JERSEY WEARERS

*ALL YOU HAVE TO DO HERE IS MATCH THE ITALIAN RIDER
WITH THE YEAR HE WORE THE YELLOW JERSEY IN LE TOUR*

911.	Flavio Vanzella	1937
912.	Claudio Chiappucci	1995
913.	Marco Pantani	1993
914.	Francesco Moser	1952
915.	Gino Bartali	1990
916.	Ivan Gotti	2000
917.	Fausto Coppi	1960
918.	Gastone Nencini	1998
919.	Alberto Elli	1994
920.	Mario Cipollini	1975

AMERICAN STAGE WINNERS

*ALL YOU HAVE TO DO HERE IS MATCH THE AMERICAN
RIDER WITH THE YEAR HE WON A STAGE IN LE TOUR*

921.	Greg Lemond	2003
922.	Davis Phinney	1995
923.	Lance Armstrong	1987
924.	Andy Hampsten	1989
925.	Lance Armstrong	1992
926.	Greg Lemond	2004
927.	Tyler Hamilton	1987
928.	Greg Lemond	2003
929.	Lance Armstrong	1985
930.	Jeff Pierce	1986

BELGIAN WINNERS OF LE TOUR

931. How many different Belgian riders have won the race - 8, 9 or 10?

932. How many Belgian riders have won Le Tour on more than 1 occasion?

933. Name any 2 of the riders in Q932.

934. Who was the last Belgian winner of Le Tour?

935. How many Belgian victories have there been in the history of Le Tour - 16, 18 or 20?

936. How many times has a Belgian rider finished in the Top 3 of a Tour de France - 18, 24 or 30?

937. How many Belgian riders have won more than 2 Tour de France?

938. Apart from the rider in Q934, name any other Belgian rider who has won more than 2 Tour de France.

939. For what Team, sponsored by a French car manufacturer, did the rider in Q938 ride when he won his first Tour de France?

940. 2 Belgian riders with the same surname have won Le Tour. What is their surname?

1996 TOUR DE FRANCE

941.   Who won Le Tour?

942.   Can you name the French rider who finished in 3rd place?

943.   What German rider won the Green Jersey?

944.   Name the French rider who won the "King of the Mountains".

945.   Can you name the Team who won the Best Team title in Le Tour
        - Festina, Kelme or TVM?

946.   What German rider and Runner-Up in Le Tour Spanish was
        awarded the White Jersey for being the Best Young Rider in Le
        Tour?

947.   Who was the highest-placed Swiss rider, finishing Le Tour in
        10th position?

948.   Who won the Final Stage on the Champs Elysées - Djamolidin
        Abdoujaparov, Fabio Baldato or Frédéric Moncassin?

949.   Can you recall the position in which Miguel Indurain finished Le
        Tour - 4th, 7th or 11th?

950.   Who was the French rider who won Stage 17 from Argeles-
        Gazost to Pampelune - Laurent Dufaux, Luc Leblanc or Richard
        Virenque?

1995 TOUR DE FRANCE

951.   Who won Le Tour?

952.   Can you name the Italian rider who finished in 5th place?

953.   What French rider won the Green Jersey?

954.   Name the French rider who won the "King of the Mountains".

955.   Can you name the Team that won the Team Time Trial - Banesto, Festina or Gewiss?

956.   What Italian rider, and future winner of Le Tour, was awarded the White Jersey for being the Best Young Rider in Le Tour?

957.   Who was the highest-placed Spanish rider, finishing Le Tour in 6th position - Vicente Apariciom, Melchor Mauri or Herminio Diaz Zabala?

958.   Who won the Final Stage on the Champs Elysées - Djamolidin Abdoujaparov, Fabio Baldato or Frédéric Moncassin?

959.   Can you recall in what position Marco Pantani finished Le Tour - 9th, 11th or 13th?

960.   2 Swiss riders finished in the overall Top 10. Name them.

1997 TOUR DE FRANCE

961. Who won Le Tour?

962. Can you name the Italian rider who finished in 3rd place?

963. What German rider won the Green Jersey?

964. Name the French rider who won the "King of the Mountains".

965. Can you name the Team who won the Best Team title in Le Tour - Festina, Mercatone Uno or Telekom?

966. What German rider was awarded the White Jersey for being the Best Young Rider in Le Tour?

967. Who was the highest-placed Spanish rider, finishing Le Tour in 4th position - Miguel Indurain, Fernando Escartin or Abraham Olano?

968. Who won the Final Stage on the Champs Elysées - Robbie McEwen, Nicola Minali or Erik Zabel?

969. Who was the highest-placed American rider?

970. Apart from the rider in Q967, 2 other Spanish riders finished in the overall Top 10. Name either of them.

GREG LEMOND

971. How many times did Greg win Le Tour?

972. In how many Tour de France did Greg participate - 6, 7 or 8?

973. In what year during the 1980s did Greg participate in his first Tour de France?

974. On how many occasions was Greg not ranked in the overall positions at the end of a Tour de France?

975. In what year did Greg win his first Tour de France - 1985, 1986 or 1987?

976. Name the Italian rider who finished Runner-Up to Greg in a Tour de France.

977. How many times did Greg win a Stage in the Tour de France - 5, 7 or 9?

978. In what year did Greg claim his first Stage victory - 1985, 1986 or 1987?

979. For what French Team did Greg ride when he won the Tour de France?

980. How many times has Greg finished in Le Tour's Final Top 5 positions?

SWISS STAGE WINNERS

ALL YOU HAVE TO DO HERE IS MATCH THE SWISS RIDER
WITH THE YEAR HE WON A STAGE IN LE TOUR

981.	Rubens Bertogliati	1996
982.	Pascal Richard	1954
983.	Fabian Cancellara	1986
984.	Tony Rominger	1996
985.	Niki Ruttmann	2002
986.	Rolf Jaermann	1986
987.	Alex Zulle	2004
988.	Erich Maechler	1993
989.	Laurent Dufaux	1992
990.	Ferdi Kubler	1996

SPANISH STAGE WINNERS

*ALL YOU HAVE TO DO HERE IS MATCH THE SPANISH
RIDER WITH THE YEAR HE WON A STAGE IN LE TOUR*

991.	Fernando Escartin	1985
992.	Juan Miguel Mercado	2003
993.	Miguel Indurain	1999
994.	Iban Mayo	1985
995.	David Etxebarria	1997
996.	Eduardo Chozas	2003
997.	Abraham Olano	2004
998.	Aitor Gonzalez	1992
999.	Carlos Sastre	1999
1000.	Pedro Delgado	2004

EXPERT - LE TOUR - 1

1001. Who was the last French rider to win Le Tour?

1002. Why did the 2003 Tour de France start and finish in Paris?

1003. In what country did the 2002 Tour de France start?

1004. What Jersey was first introduced in Le Tour in 1933?

1005. The White Jersey is awarded to the Best Young Rider in Le Tour. What is the Best Young Rider's maximum age?

1006. To the nearest 5, how many riders participated in the first Tour de France held in 1903?

1007. Who in 1909 became the first ride outside France to win Le Tour?

1008. Name either of the 2 record statistics that the 1919 Tour de France holds.

1009. To the nearest 5, what is the record number of finishers in any Tour de France?

1010. Following on from Q1009 in what year during the 1990s did this happen?

EXPERT - LE TOUR WINNERS - 1

ALL YOU HAVE TO DO HERE IS ASSOCIATE THE RIDER WITH THE YEAR HE WON LE TOUR

1011.	Bernard Hinault	1962
1012.	Greg Lemond	1968
1013.	Jacques Anquetil	1989
1014.	Bernard Thevenet	1965
1015.	Luis Ocaña	1967
1016.	Roger Pingeon	1978
1017.	Miguel Indurain	1973
1018.	Jan Janssen	1971
1019.	Eddy Merckx	1992
1020.	Felice Gimondi	1977

EXPERT - THE NEARLY MEN
1965-1974

ALL YOU HAVE TO DO HERE IS ASSOCIATE THE RIDER WITH THE YEAR HE FINISHED RUNNER-UP IN LE TOUR

1021.	Julio Jimenez	1965
1022.	Felice Gimondi	1966
1023.	Joop Zoetemelk	1967
1024.	Raymond Poulidor	1968
1025.	Bernard Thevenet	1969
1026.	Raymond Poulidor	1970
1027.	Roger Pingeon	1971
1028.	Joop Zoetemelk	1972
1029.	Jan Janssen	1973
1030.	Herman Van Springel	1974

EXPERT - COMBATIVITY WINNERS

ALL YOU HAVE TO DO HERE IS ASSOCIATE THE RIDER WITH
THE YEAR HE WON LE TOUR'S COMBATIVITY AWARD

1031.	Rik Van Looy (Belgium)	1969
1032.	Raymond Delisle (France)	1967
1033.	Eddy Merckx (Belgium)	1980
1034.	Christian Levavasseur (France)	1973
1035.	Cyrille Guimard (France)	1963
1036.	Désiré Letort (France)	1965
1037.	Gérard Saint (France)	1976
1038.	Luis Ocaña (Spain)	1968
1039.	Felice Gimondi (Italy)	1972
1040.	Roger Pingeon (France)	1959

EXPERT - TOUR RECORDS

1041. What rider has started the most Tour de France?

1042. Can you name the rider who has had the most Podium Finishes in Le Tour?

1043. How many times did the rider in Q1042 win a Podium place?

1044. What rider holds the record of most Stage wins with 35?

1045. Can you name the rider who holds the record for establishing the longest solo breakaway victory in a Stage?

1046. Name either of the 2 towns that hold the record for the fastest Stage in Le Tour.

1047. Can you recall the Italian rider who won the Stage in Q1046?

1048. Name either of the 2 towns that hold the record for the longest Stage in Le Tour, having hosted it on 2 separate occasions.

1049. In what year did the longest Tour de France take place?

1050. Who in 1922 became the first rider to win Le Tour de France without having won a Stage en route to winning the Yellow Jersey?

EXPERT - RED JERSEY WINNERS

ALL YOU HAVE TO DO HERE IS ASSOCIATE THE RIDER WITH THE YEAR HE WON LE TOUR'S INTERMEDIATE SPRINTS AWARD

1051.	Gilbert Duclos-Lassalle (France)	1971
1052.	Sean Kelly (Ireland)	1985
1053.	Gerrit Solleveld (Netherlands)	1981
1054.	Jacques Bossis (France)	1982
1055.	Jacques Hanegraaf (Netherlands)	1987
1056.	Pieter Nassen (Belgium)	1984
1057.	Frans Maassen (Netherlands)	1975
1058.	Marc Demeyer (Belgium)	1986
1059.	Freddy Maertens (Belgium)	1988
1060.	Jef Lieckens (Belgium)	1978

EXPERT - ALPE D'HUEZ
STAGE WINNERS

ALL YOU HAVE TO DO HERE IS MATCH THE RIDER WITH
THE YEAR HE WON THE STAGE TO ALPE D'HUEZ

1061.	Marco Pantani (Italy)	1952
1062.	Peter Winnen (Netherlands)	2001
1063.	Joop Zoetemelk (Netherlands)	1989
1064.	Fausto Coppi (Italy)	1981
1065.	Gianni Bugno (Italy)	1983
1066.	Peter Winnen (Netherlands)	1977
1067.	Lance Armstrong (USA)	1976
1068.	Hennie Kuiper (Netherlands)	1990
1069.	Gert-Jan Theunisse (Netherlands)	1982
1070.	Beat Breu (Switzerland)	1997

EXPERT - SHORTEST TOURS

ALL YOU HAVE TO DO HERE IS ASSOCIATE LE TOUR WITH THE
TOP 10 RANKINGS FOR THE SHORTEST EVER TOUR DE FRANCE

1071.	1990	Joint 1st
1072.	1905	7th
1073.	2001	5th
1074.	2003	Joint 1st
1075.	1904	9th
1076.	2002	10th
1077.	2004	4th
1078.	1903	8th
1079.	1988	6th
1080.	1989	3rd

EXPERT - LONGEST TOURS

ALL YOU HAVE TO DO HERE IS ASSOCIATE LE TOUR WITH THE TOP 10 RANKINGS FOR THE LOMGEST EVER TOUR DE FRANCE

1081.	1927	4th
1082.	1925	1st
1083.	1920	9th
1084.	1914	3rd
1085.	1921	10th
1086.	1924	5th
1087.	1919	8th
1088.	1923	7th
1089.	1926	6th
1090.	1928	2nd

EXPERT - THE GREEN JERSEY

1091.   Who was the first rider to actually wear the Green Jersey in Le Tour?

1092.   How many points were awarded to a Stage winner in Le Tour between 1905 and 1912?

1093.   Who was the first winner of the Green Jersey at the end of a Tour de France?

1094.   How many points are awarded to a rider in a "Stage Type I - Flat Stage" of Le Tour?

1095.   Can you name any 2 of the 3 French riders who won 2 overall Green Jersey competitions?

1096.   Name the Dutch rider who won 3 overall Green Jersey competitions.

1097.   Name the Belgian rider who won 2 overall Green Jersey competitions (1955-1956) plus 4 Unofficial Points Classification titles (1949-1952).

1098.   Who in 1957 became the first French rider to win the overall Green Jersey competition?

1099.   How many points are awarded to a rider in a "Stage Type IV - Individual Time Trial" Stage of Le Tour?

1100.   What happened to the Green Jersey in the 1988 Tour de France?

EXPERT - KING OF
THE MOUNTAINS

1101.   Who was the first Belgian winner of the "King of the Mountains"?

1102.   In what year did Richard Virenque miss out on winning 6 consecutive Polka-Dot Jerseys?

1103.   Can you name the French rider who prevented Richard Virenque from claiming 6 consecutive "King of the Mountains" titles?

1104.   This Spanish rider won 3 consecutive "King of the Mountains" titles in the 1960s. Who is he?

1105.   Can you name the rider who in 1948 won his second Polka-Dot Jersey 10 years after winning his first?

1106.   This rider is the only Spanish rider to have won Le Tour and the "King of the Mountains" title in the same year. Name him.

1107.   Can you recall the Colombian rider who won the 2000 "King of the Mountains" title?

1108.   This Dutch rider won the Polka-Dot Jersey in 1989. Who is he?

1109.   Name any 2 of the 3 Italian riders who have won 2 "King of the Mountains" titles.

1110.   This rider from Luxembourg won 7 Mountain Stages during his career. Name him.

EXPERT - EDDY MERCKX

1111.   In what year did Eddy take part in his first Tour de France?

1112.   Where did the Stage begin or end when Eddy won his first Stage in Le Tour?

1113.   When Eddy took part in his first ever Tour de France, what Team did he ride for?

1114.   In what year did Eddy claim his first Stage victory?

1115.   Eddy only finished outside Le Tour's Final Top 5 positions once in his career (1977). What overall placing did he achieve that year?

1116.   Can you name any year in which Eddy won the overall "King of the Mountains" Jersey in Le Tour?

1117.   How many times did Eddy win the Best Sprinter (Green) Jersey in Le Tour?

1118.   The most ever Stages won by Eddy in a single Tour de France was 8. He managed to do this twice. Name either year in which he achieved this remarkable feat.

1119.   In what year's Tour de France did Eddy wear the Yellow Jersey but not win it?

1120.   How many Stages did Eddy win overall in the Tour de France?

EXPERT - TIME TRIAL RECORDS

1121. What Team has set the fastest Team Time Trail in Le Tour?

1122. In what Tour de France did the first Individual Time Trial take place?

1123. What Team occupies 2 of the Top 5 places for the fastest Team Time Trials?

1124. What country was the first country to win a Team Time Trial?

1125. What Team was the first Team to win a Team Time Trial?

1126. French Teams dominated the Team Time Trials from 1983 to 1986. Name any 2 of the 4 Teams that won during this time.

1127. Can you name the Dutch rider who in 1977 was the first rider to exceed an average speed of 50 kph in a Time Trial?

1128. Who holds the Top 2 places in a Prologue in the history of Le Tour?

1129. Name the Belgian rider who in 1947 won the longest Individual Time Trial covering 139km.

1130. Can you name the Team that won 5 consecutive Team Time Trials between 1978 and 1982?

EXPERT - TOUR WINNERS OF THE 1930s

ALL YOU HAVE TO DO HERE IS ASSOCIATE THE RIDER WITH THE YEAR HE WON LE TOUR

1131.	André Leducq	1937
1132.	Sylvere Maes	1933
1133.	Roger Lapebie	1932
1134.	Antonin Magne	1930
1135.	Georges Speicher	1939
1136.	Romain Maes	1931
1137.	Antonin Magne	1938
1138.	Sylvere Maes	1934
1139.	André Leducq	1936
1140.	Gino Bartali	1935

EXPERT - LE TOUR - 2

1141. What colour of armband was given to a rider in the first Tour de France to signify that he led the race?

1142. Can you recall the name of the Italian rider who was Runner-Up in both the 1990 and 1992 Tour de France?

1143. After France, what country had the second-highest number of Teams entered in the 2004 Tour de France?

1144. Who was the first rider to win 4 consecutive Tour de France?

1145. How many Tour de France did Eddy Merckx win during the 1970s?

1146. What "Steven" finished Runner-Up in the 1988 Tour de France?

1147. What was different about the Tour de France that were held between 1930 and 1961, and those held between 1967 and 1968?

1148. How many Teams were issued with "Wild Card" invitations to the 2004 Tour de France?

1149. Name any 3 "Wild Card" Teams from the 2004 Tour de France.

1150. Who was the first Spanish rider to win Le Tour?

EXPERT - WHITE JERSEY WINNERS

ALL YOU HAVE TO DO HERE IS ASSOCIATE THE RIDER
WITH THE YEAR HE WON THE BEST YOUNG RIDER

1151.	Greg Lemond	1993
1152.	Henk Lubberding	1982
1153.	Laurent Fignon	1981
1154.	Johan Van der Velde	1998
1155.	Benoît Salmon	1984
1156.	Antonio Martín Velasco	1975
1157.	Phil Anderson	1978
1158.	Jan Ullrich	1980
1159.	Francesco Moser	1983
1160.	Peter Winnen	1999

EXPERT - BEST SPRINTERS

*ALL YOU HAVE TO DO HERE IS ASSOCIATE THE RIDER
WITH THE YEAR HE WON THE GREEN JERSEY*

1161.	Sean Kelly	1970
1162.	Jan Janssen	1962
1163.	Fritz Schär	1966
1164.	Walter Godefroot	1961
1165.	Willy Planckaert	1971
1166.	Rudi Altig	1983
1167.	Eddy Merckx	1968
1168.	Stan Ockers	1967
1169.	André Darrigade	1956
1170.	Franco Bitossi	1953

EXPERT - JACQUES ANQUETIL

1171. Name the rider who ended Jacques' winning streak of 4 consecutive Tour de France victories.

1172. Who was Runner-Up to Jacques when he won his first Tour de France?

1173. Apart from Team France, for what other Team did Jacques win a Tour de France?

1174. Name any 2 years in which Jacques won Le Tour as a member of the Team in Q1173.

1175. In what year did Jacques win his first Stage in Le Tour?

1176. What was the highest number of Stages won by Jacques in a Tour de France?

1177. Who was Runner-Up to Jacques when he won his 5th and last Tour de France?

1178. In what town did the Stage start and finish when Jacques won his first Stage in Le Tour?

1179. In what year did Jacques finish in 3rd place in Le Tour?

1180. Can you name any 1 of the 3 riders who won Le Tour between Jacques' first and second overall Yellow Jersey victories?

EXPERT - TOUR WINNERS - 2

ALL YOU HAVE TO DO HERE IS ASSOCIATE THE RIDER
WITH THE YEAR HE WON LE TOUR

1181.	Lucien Aimar	1970
1182.	Charly Gaul	1975
1183.	Bernard Hinault	1966
1184.	Jacques Anquetil	1976
1185.	Bernard Thevenet	1960
1186.	Louison Bobet	1963
1187.	Gastone Nencini	1949
1188.	Eddy Merckx	1958
1189.	Fausto Coppi	1955
1190.	Lucien Van Impe	1985

EXPERT - LE TOUR "FIRSTS"

1191. Who won the very first Tour in 1903 - Jean Garin, Maurice Garin or Phillipe Garin?

1192. Who was the first rider to win 5 Tour de France?

1193. Who was the first rider to successfully defend his Tour de France title?

1194. What French car manufacturer was the first to sponsor a winner of Le Tour?

1195. Who in 1912 became the first Belgian rider to win Le Tour?

1196. Can you recall the name of the rider who was the first man to finish Runner-Up in Le Tour and then win it the following year?

1197. What country did Francois Faber, the first non-French winner of Le Tour in 1912, come from?

1198. Who was the first Italian rider to win Le Tour?

1199. In what year was Le Tour not held for the first time since it began in 1903?

1200. Who was the first rider to win 3 consecutive Tour de France?

EXPERT - THE NEARLY MEN
1975-1984

*ALL YOU HAVE TO DO HERE IS ASSOCIATE THE RIDER
WITH THE YEAR HE FINISHED RUNNER-UP IN LE TOUR*

1201.	Joop Zoetemelk	1975
1202.	Lucien Van Impe	1976
1203.	Joop Zoetemelk	1977
1204.	Bernard Hinault	1978
1205.	Hennie Kuiper	1979
1206.	Angel Arroyo	1980
1207.	Joop Zoetemelk	1981
1208.	Eddy Merckx	1982
1209.	Hennie Kuiper	1983
1210.	Joop Zoetemelk	1984

EXPERT - TIME TRIALS

*ALL YOU HAVE TO DO HERE IS ASSOCIATE THE TIME
TRIAL WITH THE YEAR IT HAPPENED IN LE TOUR*

1211. Chris Boardman (GB)
sets the fastest ever Prologue   2000

1212. Gewiss (Italy) set the fastest Team Time Trial   2003

1213. Lance Armstrong (USA) records the 2nd
fastest ever time in an Individual Team
Time Trial over 30km   1987

1214. Greg Lemond (USA) sets the fastest ever time
in an Individual Team Time Trial between
10-30km   1995

1215. Fabian Cancellara (Spain) records the 3rd
fastest ever Prologue   1998

1216. Carreras (Italy) set the 2nd record the 2nd fastest
ever [SENSE?] Team Time Trial   1994

1217. Chris Boardman (GB) sets the 2nd fastest
ever Prologue   1954

1218. David Millar (GB) sets the fastest ever time
in an Individual Team Time Trial over 30km   2000

1219. Switzerland win the first ever Individual
Team Time Trial   2004

1220. Jan Ullrich (Germany) records the 3rd fastest
ever time in an Individual Team Time Trial
over 30km   1989

EXPERT - LONGEST SOLO RIDES IN LE TOUR

ALL YOU HAVE TO DO HERE IS ASSOCIATE THE RIDER WITH HIS TOP 10 PLACING AND SOLO RIDE DISTANCE/YEAR IN LE TOUR

1221.	Régis Clère (France)	182.5km (10)	1993
1222.	Bernard Quilfen (France)	253km (1)	1947
1223.	Thierry Marie (France)	193km (8)	1968
1224.	Marcel Dussault (France)	214km (5)	1950
1225.	Albert Bourlon (France)	189.5km (9)	1987
1226.	Fabio Roscioli (Italy)	205km (6)	1966
1227.	Pierre Beuffeuil (France)	234km (2)	1991
1228.	José Perez Frances (Spain)	200km (7)	1950
1229.	Roger Pingeon (France)	222km (4)	1977
1230.	Maurice Blomme (Belgium)	223km (3)	1963

EXPERT - TOUR WINNERS OF THE 1950s

ALL YOU HAVE TO DO HERE IS ASSOCIATE THE RIDER WITH THE YEAR HE WON LE TOUR

1231.	Fausto Coppi	1956
1232.	Jacques Anquetil	1950
1233.	Louison Bobet	1952
1234.	Ferdy Kubler	1955
1235.	Roger Walkowiak	1951
1236.	Louison Bobet	1959
1237.	Federico Bahamontes	1953
1238.	Charly Gaul	1954
1239.	Hugo Koblet	1958
1240.	Louison Bobet	1957

EXPERT - LANCE ARMSTRONG

1241. In what year did Lance participate in his first Tour de France?

1242. Name any 2 of the 3 years that Lance was not ranked in the overall positions at the end of a Tour de France?

1243. In what final position did Lance finish in the 1995 Tour de France - 6th, 36th or 66th?

1244. Name the rider who finished Runner-Up to Lance when he won his first Tour de France in 1999.

1245. How many Stages did Lance win on his way to victory in the 2001 Tour de France?

1246. How many times has Lance won a Stage in the Tour de France?

1247. Where did the Stage begin or end when Lance won his first ever Stage in Le Tour?

1248. In how many of the Tour de France entered by Lance Armstrong has he failed to win a Stage?

1249. Name any year in which Lance has failed to win a Stage in the Tour de France.

1250. Apart from the Yellow Jersey, what other colour of "Leaders Jersey" (not Team) did Lance wear in both the 1999 and 2002 Tour de France?

ANSWERS

2004 - LE TOUR - 1

1. Belgium
2. 21
3. Lance Armstrong
4. 20 plus 1 Prologue
5. 189
6. Stage 10 (Limoges to St Flour, 237km)
7. Richard Virenque
8. 3,395km
9. 11
10. 40.553 km/h

LANCE ARMSTRONG

11. 6
12. 10
13. Jan Ullrich
14. Motorola
15. 3
16. 1999
17. Joseba Beloki
18. Austin
19. 1993
20. 4

KNOW YOUR NATIONALITY - 1

21.	Daniele Nardello	Italian
22.	Greg Lemond	American
23.	Fernando Escartin	Spanish
24.	Bjarne Riis	Danish
25.	Stephen Roche	Irish
26.	Tom Steels	Belgian
27.	Lauren Fignon	French
28.	Chris Boardman	English
29.	Jacques Anquetil	French
30.	Francisco Mancebo	Spanish

FASTEST TOURS

31.	Lance Armstrong:	2002	6th
32.	Lance Armstrong:	1999	3rd
33.	Miguel Indurain:	1995	10th
34.	Lance Armstrong:	2000	7th
35.	Marco Pantani:	1998	5th
36.	Bjarne Riis:	1996	9th
37.	Lance Armstrong:	2003	1st
38.	Miguel Indurain:	1992	8th
39.	Lance Armstrong:	2004	2nd
40.	Lance Armstrong:	2001	4th

1960s TOUR WINNERS

41.	Lucien Aimar	1966
42.	Jacques Anquetil	1961
43.	Jan Janssen	1968
44.	Gastone Nencini	1960
45.	Jacques Anquetil	1962
46.	Felice Gimondi	1965
47.	Eddy Merckx	1969
48.	Jacques Anquetil	1963
49.	Roger Pingeon	1967
50.	Jacques Anquetil	1964

EDDY MERCKX

51.	Belgian
52.	5
53.	1969-1972 & 1974
54.	7
55.	Joop Zoetemelk
56.	None (he was always ranked)
57.	Raymond Poulidor
58.	Green (Best Sprinter) & Polka-Dot (King of the Mountains)
59.	8 (on 2 occasions)
60.	4

FOREIGN STARTS FOR LE TOUR

61.	Luxembourg	2002
62.	Holland	1978
63.	Belgium	1958
64.	Spain	1992

65.	Germany	1987
66.	Ireland	1998
67.	Switzerland	1982
68.	Belgium	2004
69.	Holland	1954
70.	Germany	1980

KING OF THE MOUNTAINS WINNERS - 1

71.	Claudio Chiappucci	1991
72.	Richard Virenque	2004
73.	Tony Rominger	1993
74.	Thierry Claveyrolat	1990
75.	Bernard Hinault	1986
76.	Pedro Torres	1973
77.	Eddy Merckx	1970
78.	Christophe Rinero	1998
79.	Lucien Van Impe	1977
80.	Luis Herrera	1985

LE TOUR - 1

81.	1903
82.	Pedro Delgado
83.	Marco Pantani (1998)
84.	Dublin
85.	White
86.	Lance Armstrong
87.	Red & White Polka-Dot
88.	Holland (The Netherlands)
89.	Luxembourg
90.	Jan Ullrich

JACQUES ANQUETIL

91.	8
92.	1957
93.	2
94.	5
95.	1957 & 1961-1964
96.	16
97.	5
98.	2
99.	Team France

100.   Italian (Felice Gimondi)

2003 TOUR DE FRANCE

101.   Lance Armstroing
102.   Tyler Hamilton
103.   Baden Cooke
104.   Richard Virenque
105.   Ivan Basso
106.   Denis Menchov
107.   Christophe Moreau
108.   US Postal
109.   Haimar Zubeldia (5th) & Iban Mayo (6th)
110.   Jean-Patrick Nazon

LUIS OCANA

111.   Spanish
112.   8
113.   1969
114.   4
115.   1973
116.   Bernard Thevenet
117.   9
118.   1970
119.   6
120.   1 (1973 - the year he won it)

LE TOUR RECORDS

121.   8 seconds
122.   Greg Lemond's winning margin over Laurent Fignon in 1989
123.   Raymond Poulidor
124.   Chris Boardman
125.   28 minutes, 27seconds
126.   Fausto Coppi (over Stan Ockers in 1952)
127.   Eddy Merckx
128.   8
129.   Charles Pelissier (1930), Eddy Merckx (1970 & 1974) & Freddy Maertens (1976)
130.   Joop Zoetemelk

LE TOUR WINNERS BY COUNTRY

131.   Italy   9

132.	Switzerland	2
133.	France	36
134.	Ireland	1
135.	Spain	8
136.	Holland	2
137.	Luxembourg	4
138.	Germany	1
139.	Belgium	18
140.	USA	9

BEST SPRINTER WINNERS - 1

141.	Sean Kelly	1989
142.	Djamolidin Abdoujaparov	1993
143.	Eddy Merckx	1972
144.	Baden Cooke	2003
145.	Erik Zabel	1999
146.	Robbie McEwen	2004
147.	Freddy Maertens	1976
148.	Laurent Jalabert	1995
149.	Eric Vanderaerden	1986
150.	Bernard Hinault	1979

2004 TEAM LEADERS

151.	Lance Armstrong	US Postal
152.	Christophe Moreau	Crédit Agricole
153.	Robbie McEwen	Lotto-Domo
154.	Jan Ullrich	T-Mobile
155.	Michael Boogard	Rabobank
156.	Iban Mayo	Euskaltel-Euskadi
157.	Stuart O'Grady	Cofidis
158.	Richard Virenque	Quick Step
159.	Francisco Mancebo	Illes Balears-Banesto
160.	Ivan Basso	CSC

THE NEARLY MEN 1985-1994

161.	Steven Rooks	1988
162.	Gianni Bugno	1991
163.	Greg Lemond	1985
164.	Claudio Chiappucci	1992
165.	Piotr Ugramov	1994
166.	Tony Rominger	1993

167.	Pedro Delgado	1987
168.	Laurent Fignon	1989
169.	Claudio Chiappucci	1990
170.	Bernard Hinault	1986

ROGER PINGEON

171. French
172. 8
173. 1965
174. Eddy Merckx
175. 2 (1970 & 1972)
176. 1967
177. No
178. 4
179. 1968 & 1969
180. 1 (1967, the year he won it)

TOUR WINNERS - 1

181.	Lance Armstrong	2003
182.	Miguel Indurain	1994
183.	Jacques Anquetil	1961
184.	Lauren Fignon	1983
185.	Eddy Merckx	1974
186.	Stephen Roche	1987
187.	Bernard Hinault	1979
188.	Greg Lemond	1990
189.	Fausto Coppi	1952
190.	Bjarne Riis	1996

THE RED JERSEY

191. Intermediate Sprints Classification
192. 1971
193. Pieter Nassen
194. Belgian
195. Sean Kelly
196. 1982, 1983 & 1989
197. Barry Hoban
198. 1984
199. Dutch (Jacques Hanegraaf)
200. 1989 (to Sean Kelly of Ireland)

MOST STAGE WINS IN LE TOUR

201.	Jean Alavoine (France)	17
202.	André Leducq (France)	25
203.	Jacques Anquetil (France)	16
204.	André Darrigade (France)	22
205.	Eddy Merckx (Belgium)	35
206.	Nicolas Frantz (Luxembourg)	20
207.	François Faber (Luxembourg)	19
208.	Bernard Hinault (France)	28
209.	René Le Greves (France)	16
210.	Lance Armstrong (USA)	21

STEPHEN ROCHE

211. Irish
212. 10
213. 1983
214. 2 (1989 & 1991)
215. 1987
216. Pedro Delgado
217. 3
218. 1985
219. Carrera
220. 2 (1985 & 1987)

RUSSIAN RIDERS

221. Viatcheslav Ekimov
222. Dimitri Konyshev
223. Vladimir Karpets
224. Dimitri Zhdanov
225. Evgueni Berzin
226. Viatcheslav Ekimov (Stage 4)
227. 4
228. Alexei Sivakov
229. Vladislav Bobrik
230. Dimitri Konyshev (Pav in 1990)

TEAM TIME TRIAL WINNERS - 1

231.	1982	Raleigh (Netherlands)
232.	1984	Renault (France)
233.	1986	Système 'U' (France)
234.	1990	Panasonic (Netherlands)

236.	1991	Ariostea (Italy)
236.	1993	GB-MG (Italy)
237.	1995	Gewiss (Italy)
238.	2002	ONCE (Spain)
239.	2003	US Postal Service (USA)
240.	1977	Fiat (Belgium)

TOUR JARGON

241.	Domestique	A rider who willingly sacrifices their own chances of winning Le Tour and works in every Stage to help their Team leaders
242.	Étape	A Stage in Le Tour
243.	Maillot Jaune	The yellow jersey worn by the leading rider in Le Tour
244.	Parcours	The description for the route that Le Tour takes each day
245.	Peloton	The name associated with the main bunch of riders
246.	Contre La Montre	The Time Trial
247.	Tête de la Course	The front of the race
248.	Hors Catégorie	The toughest climb in any Mountain Stage of Le Tour
249.	Équipe	A Team in Le Tour
250.	Directeur Sportif	The Manager of a Team in Le Tour

BERNARD THEVENET

251. 2
252. 1975 & 1977
253. 11
254. 1970
255. 3
256. Eddy Merckx
257. 9
258. 1970
259. Peugeot (and also for his 2nd victory)
260. 1 (to Luis Ocaña in 1973)

HISTORY OF LE TOUR

261. L'Auto
262. 20,000 francs
263. Red (The "Lanterne Rouge")
264. Lyon
265. 20
266. Mountain

267. 1 kilometre to the end of the Stage
268. A race number
269. The magazine was printed on yellow paper
270. An armband

2004 - LE TOUR - 2

271. 6
272. Liege
273. Robbie McEwen
274. Tom Boonen
275. 2 Individual plus 1 Team Time Trial
276. 400,000 euros
277. Andreas Kloden
278. 147
279. 6
280. Will Smith

KNOW YOUR NATIONALITY - 2

281. Richard Virenque   French
282. Abraham Olano   Spanish
283. Laurent Jalabert   French
284. Marco Pantani   Italian
285. Jan Ullrich   German
286. Lance Armstrong   American
287. Robbie McEwen   Australian
288. Alex Zulle   Swiss
289. Eddy Merckx   Belgian
290. Miguel Indurain   Spanish

1970s TOUR WINNERS

291. Eddy Merckx   1970
292. Bernard Hinault   1978
293. Luis Ocaña   1973
294. Bernard Thevenet   1977
295. Eddy Merckx   1974
296. Lucien Van Impe   1976
297. Eddy Merckx   1971
298. Bernard Hinault   1979
299. Eddy Merckx   1972
300. Bernard Thevenet   1975

COMBATIVITY WINNERS - 1

301.	Laurent Jalabert (France)	2001
302.	Massimo Ghirotto (Italy)	1993
303.	Bernard Hinault (France)	1986
304.	Richard Virenque (France)	2004
305.	Claudio Chiappucci (Italy)	1992
306.	Jérôme Simon (France)	1988
307.	Alexandre Vinokourov (Kaz)	2003
308.	Jacky Durand (France)	1999
309.	Hernán Buenahora (Colombia)	1995
310.	Laurent Fignon (France)	1989

LAURENT JALABERT

311.	French
312.	Green (1992)
313.	4th
314.	1995
315.	2
316.	1995 & 2000
317.	2
318.	1992 & 1995
319.	4
320.	4

MOST TOURS PARTICIPATED IN

321.	Raymond Poulidor (France)	14
322.	Guy Nulens (Belgium)	15
323.	Joop Zoetemelk (Netherlands)	16
324.	André Darrigade (France)	14
325.	Joaquim Agostinho (Portugal)	13
326.	Sean Kelly (Ireland)	14
327.	Lucien Van Impe (Belgium)	15
328.	Jules Deloffre (France)	14
329.	Phil Anderson (Australia)	13
330.	Viatcheslav Ekimov (Russia)	14

LE TOUR - 2

331.	Gianni Bugno
332.	Holland (The Netherlands)
333.	Green
334.	Bernard Hinault

335. Greg Lemond (1986)
336. Alex Zulle
337. Raleigh
338. Bjarne Riis
339. Stephen Roche
340. 5 (1981-1985)

1999 TOUR DE FRANCE

341. Lance Armstrong
342. Alex Zulle
343. Erik Zabel
344. Richard Virenque
345. Benoît Salmon
346. Mario Cipollini
347. Jann Kirispuu
348. Bobby Julich
349. A fan stood on the road in front of him to take a photo
350. David Etxebarria

TEAM TIME TRIAL WINNERS - 2

351.	2001	Crédit Agricole (France)
352.	1983	Coöp-Mercier (France)
353.	1989	Super 'U' (France)
354.	2004	US Postal Service (USA)
355.	1994	GB-MG (Italy)
356.	1992	Panasonic (Netherlands)
357.	1981	Raleigh (Netherlands)
358.	2000	ONCE (Spain)
359.	1985	La Vie Claire (France)
360.	1987	Carrera (Italy)

WHAT TEAM DID I RIDE FOR?

361.	Lance Armstrong	US Postal
362.	Jan Ullrich	T-Mobile
363.	Iban Mayo	Euskaltel/Euskadi
364.	Francisco Mancebo	Illes Balears.com
365.	Thor Hushovd	Crédit Agricole
366.	Jean-Patrick Nazon	AG2R
367.	Stuart O'Grady	Cofidis
368.	Robbie McEwen	Lotto/Domo
369.	Ivan Basso	CSC World Online

370.	Richard Virenque	Quick Step

WHITE JERSEY WINNERS - 1

371.	Marco Pantani	1994
372.	Ivan Basso	2002
373.	Erik Breukink	1988
374.	Oscar Sevilla	2001
375.	Raúl Alcala	1987
376.	Vladimir Karpets	2004
377.	Alvaro Mejía	1991
378.	Jan Ullrich	1997
379.	Enrique Martínez Heredia	1976
380.	Eddy Bouwmans	1992

THE GREEN JERSEY

381.	Hope
382.	1953
383.	Greengrocers
384.	Eddy Merckx & Freddy Maertens
385.	Swiss
386.	Djamolidin Abdoujaparov
387.	4
388.	Type I: Flat Stage, Type II: Semi-Mountainous Stage, Type III: Mountainous Stage & Type IV: Individual Time Trials
389.	Erik Zabel (1996-2001)
390.	Sean Kelly (1982, 1983, 1985 & 1989)

MIGUEL INDURAIN

391.	12
392.	1985
393.	2 (1985 & 1986)
394.	5
395.	1991-1995
396.	12
397.	1989
398.	Gianni Bugno (1991), Claudio Chiappucci (1992), Tony Rominger (1993), Piotr Ugramov (1994) & Alex Zulle (1995)
399.	Banesto
400.	Greg Lemond & Bjarne Riis

RUNNER-UP AND WINNER IN CONSECUTIVE YEARS

401.	Nicolas Frantz	1926 & 1927
402.	Bernard Hinault	1984 & 1985
403.	Francois Faber	1908 & 1909
404.	Ottavio Bottecchia	1923 & 1924
405.	Pedro Delgado	1987 & 1988
406.	Joop Zoetemelk	1979 & 1980
407.	Lucien Buysse	1925 & 1926
408.	Greg Lemond	1985 & 1986
409.	Jan Ullrich	1996 & 1997
410.	Jan Janssen	1966 & 1968

2004 STAGE WINNERS

411.	Prologue	Fabian Cancellara
412.	Stage 1	Jann Kirsipuu
413.	Stage 5	Stuart O'Grady
414.	Stage 7	Filippo Pozzato
415.	Stage 8	Thor Hushovd
416.	Stage 11	David Moncoutie
417.	Stage 12	Ivan Basso
418.	Stage 14	Aitor Gonzalez
419.	Stage 16	Lance Armstrong
420.	Stage 18	Juan Miguel Mercado

THE POLKA-DOT JERSEY

421.	The "King of the Mountains" (Best Climber)
422.	1933
423.	Spanish (Vicente Trueba)
424.	1975
425.	Poulain (a chocolate manufacturer)
426.	The wrappers of the chocolate were polka-dot
427.	Richard Virenque (with 7)
428.	Dutch (Joop Zoetemelk - 1980 winner)
429.	The Alps & Pyrenees
430.	Luis Herrera

KNOW YOUR NATIONALITY - 3

431.	Steve Bauer	Canadian
432.	Joseba Beloki	Spanish
433.	Viatcheslav Ekimov	Russian
434.	George Hincapie	American

435.	Erik Zabel	German
436.	Santiago Botero	Colombian
437.	Bernard Hinault	French
438.	Sean Kelly	Irish
439.	Roberto Heras	Spanish
440.	Tyler Hamilton	American

JAN ULLRICH

441.	German
442.	7
443.	1996
444.	None (he has always been ranked)
445.	1997
446.	Richard Virenque
447.	7
448.	1996
449.	Telekom
450.	7 (1996-1998, 2000-2001 & 2003-2004)

2000 TOP 10 FINISHERS

451.	Daniele Nardello (Italy), Mapei-Quick Step	10
452.	Fernando Escartin (Spain), Kelme-Costa Blanca	8
453.	Francisco Mancebo (Spain), Banesto	9
454.	Richard Virenque (France), Team Polti	6
455.	Christophe Moreau (France), Festina	4
456.	Joseba Beloki (Spain), Festina	3
457.	Lance Armstrong (USA), US Postal Service	1
458.	Jan Ullrich (Germany), Team Deutsche Telekom	2
459.	Santiago Botero (Columbia), Kelme-Costa Blanca	7
460.	Roberto Heras (Spain), Kelme-Costa Blanca	5

1980s TOUR WINNERS

461.	Pedro Delgado	1988
462.	Bernard Hinault	1981
463.	Greg Lemond	1989
464.	Laurent Fignon	1984
465.	Bernard Hinault	1982
466.	Joop Zoetemelk	1980
467.	Greg Lemond	1986
468.	Bernard Hinault	1985
469.	Stephen Roche	1987

470.	Laurent Fignon	1983

SEAN KELLY

471.	Irish
472.	4th
473.	1985
474.	1
475.	4
476.	1982, 1983, 1985 & 1989
477.	5
478.	2 (1987 & 1991)
479.	1978
480.	1982

KING OF THE MOUNTAINS

481.	Richard Virenque
482.	Eddy Merckx
483.	He was the first rider to win the Yellow & Polka-Dot Jerseys
484.	René Vietto
485.	Federico Bahamontes
486.	Tony Rominger
487.	Lucien Van Impe
488.	Robert Millar
489.	Claudio Chiappucci
490.	Steven Rooks

LE TOUR STAGE FINISHES

491.	Nantes	28
492.	Briançon	30
493.	Metz	37
494.	Bordeaux	78
495.	Marseille	32
496.	Pau	54
497.	Caen	33
498.	Paris	96
499.	Bayonne	30
500.	Bagnères-de-Luchon	45

PEDRO DELGADO

501.	Spanish
502.	11

503.	1983
504.	1 (1984)
505.	1988
506.	Steven Rooks
507.	4
508.	1985
509.	Reynolds
510.	1

2000 TOUR DE FRANCE

511.	Lance Armstrong
512.	2
513.	Erik Zabel
514.	Santiago Botero
515.	Francisco Mancebo
516.	David Millar
517.	Tom Steels
518.	ONCE
519.	Stage 10 (Lourdes to Hautacam)
520.	Erik Zabel

THE NEARLY MEN 1995-2004

521.	1995	Alex Zulle
522.	1996	Jan Ullrich
523.	1997	Richard Virenque
524.	1998	Jan Ullrich
525.	1999	Alex Zulle
526.	2000	Jan Ullrich
527.	2001	Jan Ullrich
528.	2002	Joseba Beloki
529.	2003	Jan Ullrich
530.	2004	Andreas Kloden

2004 TEAM MANAGERS

531.	Johan Bruyneel	US Postal
532.	Roger Legeay	Crédit Agricole
533.	Marc Sergeant	Lotto-Domo
534.	Walter Godefroot	T-Mobile
535.	Theo de Rooy	Rabobank
536.	Miguel Madariaga	Euskaltel-Euskadi
537.	Cyrille Guimard	Cofidis

538.	Alvaro Crespi	Quick Step
539.	José-Miguel Echavarri	Illes Balears-Banesto
540.	Bjarne Riis	CSC

BJARNE RIIS

541.	Danish
542.	9
543.	1989
544.	1 (1990)
545.	1996
546.	Jan Ullrich
547.	4
548.	1993
549.	Deutsche Telekom
550.	3 (1993, 1995 & 1996)

2004 - LE TOUR - 3

551.	Lance Armstrong
552.	Vladimir Karpets
553.	Illes Balears
554.	Thomas Voeckler
555.	Erik Zabel
556.	T-Mobile (248 hrs, 58 mins, 43 secs)
557.	35
558.	Quick Step
559.	The Discovery Channel
560.	4th

LUCIEN AIMAR

561.	French
562.	1
563.	9
564.	1965
565.	1 (1965)
566.	Jan Janssen (1968 winner)
567.	1 (1967)
568.	Ford
569.	4
570.	Never

SPANISH RIDERS

571. Eduardo Chozas
572. José-Luis Viejo
573. Joseba Beloki
574. José de Los Angeles
575. Pedro Delgado
576. Miguel Indurain
577. Javier Murguialday
578. 2 (Stages 12 & 16)
579. Federico Echave
580. Julio Jimenez

KNOW YOUR NATIONALITY - 4

581.	Richard Virenque	French
582.	Bobby Julich	American
583.	Joseba Beloki	Spanish
584.	Jacky Durand	French
585.	Mario Cipollini	Italian
586.	Pedro Delgado	Spanish
587.	Baden Cooke	Australian
588.	Ivan Basso	Italian
589.	Santiago Botero	Colombian
590.	Erik Dekker	Dutch

JOOP ZOETEMELK

591. Dutch
592. 16
593. 1970
594. None (he was always ranked)
595. 1980
596. Hennie Kuiper
597. 10
598. 1973
599. TI-Raleigh
600. 11 (1970-1973, 1975-1976 & 1978-1982)

LE TOUR INCIDENTS

601.	Tom Simpson dies during the climb of Mont Ventoux.	1967
602.	Adolphe Helière dives into the sea on a rest day and drowns.	1910
603.	Tour photographers go on strike.	1987
604.	Fans protest by throwing nails in the streets.	1905

605.	Fabio Casartelli falls off his bike descending the Portet d'Aspet and hits his head on a stone. He is taken to hospital and dies there.	1985
606.	Francisco Cepeda dies after breaking his skull after falling off his bike.	1935
607.	Riders protest over early start times in Le Tour.	1978
608.	Riders object angrily to Le Tour's first doping tests.	1966
609.	Riders react angrily to police raids and the treatment by the police of members of the TVM Team.	1998
610.	Journalists block the road during Le Tour.	1968

SPONSORS 2004 TOUR

611. Skoda
612. Crédit Lyonnias, Nestlé Aquarel, Skoda Auto & Supermarché Champion
613. Nike
614. Kawasaki
615. PMU
616. Michelin
617. Floor Berry
618. Supermarché Champion
619. Crédit Lyonnais
620. Disneyland

THE TOP 10 OF 2004

621.	Carlos Sastre	8
622.	José Azevedo	5
623.	Andreas Kloden	2
624.	Lance Armstrong	1
625.	Georg Totschnig	7
626.	Ivan Basso	3
627.	Levi Leipheimer	9
628.	Francisco Mancebo	6
629.	Oscar Pereiro	10
630.	Jan Ullrich	4

BEST SPRINTER WINNERS - 2

631.	Rik Van Linden	1975
632.	Djamolidin Abdoujaparov	1994
633.	Jacques Esclassan	1977
634.	Eddy Merckx	1971
635.	Jean-Paul Van Poppel	1987
636.	Laurent Jalabert	1992

637.	Erik Zabel	2000
638.	Freddy Maertens	1981
639.	Robbie McEwen	2002
640.	Sean Kelly	1982

2001 TOUR DE FRANCE

641. Lance Armstrong
642. Joseba Beloki
643. Erik Zabel
644. Laurent Jalabert
645. Erik Dekker
646. Oscar Sevilla
647. Francois Simon
648. Crédit Agricole
649. Jann Kirsipuu
650. Oscar Sevilla (7th) & Santiago Botero (8th)

LUCIEN VAN IMPE

651. Belgian
652. 1
653. 15
654. 1969
655. None (he was always ranked)
656. Joop Zoetemelk (1980 winner)
657. 9
658. King of the Mountains
659. 6 (1971, 1972, 1975, 1977, 1981 & 1983)
660. 1 (1981)

COMBATIVITY WINNERS - 2

661.	Bernard Hinault (France)	1984
662.	Erik Dekker (Netherlands)	2000
663.	Richard Virenque (France)	1997
664.	Eduardo Chozas (Spain)	1990
665.	Jacky Durand (France)	1998
666.	Claudio Chiappucci (Italy)	1991
667.	Eros Poli (Italy)	1994
668.	Maarten Ducrot (Netherlands)	1985
669.	Laurent Jalabert (France)	2002
670.	Pedro Delgado (Spain)	1987

LE TOUR - 3

671. Dutch, Irish, Spanish & American
672. Bernard Hinault
673. Renault
674. 2003 (40.940 km/hr)
675. Joop Zoetemelk (1980)
676. 6 mins, 19 secs
677. Andreas Kloden
678. Lance Armstrong (6), Jacques Anquetil (5), Bernard Hinault (5), Miguel Indurain (5) & Eddy Merckx (5)
679. Richard Virenque (he won the "King of the Mountains")
680. Bjarne Riis

WHITE JERSEY WINNERS - 2

681.	Jan Ullrich	1996
682.	Jean-René Bernaudeau	1979
683.	Denis Menchov	2003
684.	Fabio Parra	1985
685.	Gilles Delion	1990
686.	Dietrich Thurau	1977
687.	Marco Pantani	1995
688.	Fabrice Philipot	1989
689.	Francisco Mancebo	2000
690.	Andrew Hampsten	1986

MARCO PANTANI

691. Italian
692. 5
693. 1994
694. 1 (2000)
695. 1998
696. Jan Ullrich
697. 8
698. 1995
699. Mercatone Uno
700. 3 (1994, 1997 & 1998)

KING OF THE MOUNTAINS WINNERS - 2

701.	Domingo Perurena	1974
702.	Santiago Botero	2000
703.	Stephen Rooks	1988

704.	Mariano Martinez	1978
705.	Robert Millar	1984
706.	Claudio Chiappucci	1992
707.	Giancarlo Bellini	1976
708.	Richard Virenque	1999
709.	Lucien Van Impe	1971
710.	Luis Herrera	1987

THE TOP 10 OF 2004 - 2

711.	Carlos Sastre	CSC
712.	José Azevedo	US Postal
713.	Andreas Kloden	T-Mobile
714.	Lance Armstrong	US Postal
715.	Georg Totschnig	Gerolsteiner
716.	Ivan Basso	CSC
717.	Levi Leipheimer	Rabobank
718.	Francisco Mancebo	Illes Balears
719.	Oscar Pereiro	Phonak
720.	Jan Ullrich	T-Mobile

JAN JANSSEN

721.	Dutch
722.	8
723.	1963
724.	1 (in his first Tour de France)
725.	1968
726.	Best Sprinter (Green Jersey)
727.	3 (1964, 1965 & 1967)
728.	7
729.	2 (1964 & 1968)
730.	3 (1966-1968)

MOST YELLOW JERSEYS IN LE TOUR

731.	Miguel Indurain (Spain)	60
732.	André Leducq (France)	35
733.	Jacques Anquetil (France)	51
734.	Ottavio Bottecchia (Italy)	33
735.	Antonin Magne (France)	39
736.	Eddy Merckx (Belgium)	96
737.	Nicolas Frantz (Luxembourg)	37
738.	Louison Bobet (France)	34

| 739. | Bernard Hinault (France) | 79 |
| 740. | Lance Armstrong (USA) | 66 |

RICHARD VIRENQUE

741.	French
742.	2nd
743.	1997
744.	2
745.	1992 & 2003
746.	7
747.	1994-1997, 1999, 2003-2004
748.	7
749.	1
750.	1994

FRENCH WINNERS OF LE TOUR

751.	21
752.	8
753.	Laurent Fignon
754.	1989
755.	36
756.	Bernard Hinault
757.	1985
758.	3
759.	Jacques Anquetil (5), Bernard Hinault (5) & Louison Bobet (3)
760.	Laurent Fignon

TOUR WINNERS - 2

761.	Marco Pantani	1998
762.	Joop Zoetemelk	1980
763.	Lance Armstrong	1999
764.	Bernard Hinault	1982
765.	Eddy Merckx	1972
766.	Pedro Delgado	1988
767.	Greg Lemond	1986
768.	Lauren Fignon	1984
769.	Miguel Indurain	1993
770.	Jan Ullrich	1997

2002 TOUR DE FRANCE

| 771. | Lance Armstrong |

772. Santiago Botero
773. Robbie McEwen
774. Laurent Jalabert
775. Ivan Basso
776. Joseba Beloki
777. David Moncoutié
778. ONCE
779. Joseba Beloki (2nd), Igor González de Galdeano (5th) & José Azevedo (6th)
780. Axel Merckx

LAURENT FIGNON

781. 2
782. 1983 & 1984
783. 10
784. 1983
785. 4
786. Bernard Hinault
787. 9
788. 1983
789. Renault (and also for his 2nd victory)
790. 1 (to Greg Lemond in 1989)

1990 TOUR DE FRANCE

791. Greg Lemond
792. Claudio Chiappucci
793. Olaf Ludwig
794. Thierry Claveyrolat
795. Erik Breukink
796. Z (France)
797. Gilles Delion
798. Steve Bauer, Claudio Chiappucci, Thierry Marie & Ronan Pensec
799. Eduardo Chozas
800. Miguel Indurain (he won the next 5 Tour de France)

ROBBIE McEWEN

801. Australian
802. 89th
803. 1998
804. 1 (2004)
805. 1999
806. 2

807. 2002
808. 5
809. 0 (he has always been ranked)
810. Paris-Champs-Elysées (Stage 20: Arpajon to Paris-Champs-Elysées)

SPANISH PODIUM APPEARANCES

811.	Miguel Indurain	1991 (1st)
812.	Luis Ocaña	1973 (1st)
813.	Julio Jimenez	1967 (2nd)
814.	Pedro Delgado	1988 (1st)
815.	Angel Arroyo	1983 (2nd)
816.	Federico Bahamontes	1959 (1st)
817.	Bernardo Ruiz	1952 (3rd)
818.	Vicente Lopez-Carril	1974 (3rd)
819.	José Perez-Frances	1963 (3rd)
820.	José-Manuel Fuente	1973 (3rd)

ITALIAN PODIUM APPEARANCES

821.	Gino Bartali	1938 (1st)
822.	Marco Pantani	1998 (1st)
823.	Gianni Motta	1965 (3rd)
824.	Franco Balmamion	1967 (3rd)
825.	Claudio Chiappucci	1990 (2nd)
826.	Gastone Nencini	1960 (1st)
827.	Guido Carlesi	1961 (2nd)
828.	Felice Gimondi	1965 (1st)
829.	Gianni Bugno	1992 (3rd)
830.	Fausto Coppi	1949 (1st)

FAUSTO COPPI

831. Italian
832. 2
833. 1949 & 1952
834. 3
835. Gino Bartali
836. Best Climber (King of the Mountains - 1949 & 1952)
837. 9
838. 10th (1951)
839. 5 (1952)
840. Team Italy (in both his Tour de France victories)

ALPE D'HUEZ STAGE WINNERS

841.	Roberto Conti (Italy)	1994
842.	Iban Mayo (Spain)	2003
843.	Bernard Hinault (France)	1986
844.	Andrew Hampsten (USA)	1992
845.	Luis Herrera (Colombia)	1984
846.	Stephen Rooks (Netherlands)	1988
847.	Lance Armstrong (USA)	2004
848.	Giuseppe Guerini (Italy)	1999
849.	Federico Echave (Spain)	1987
850.	Gianni Bugno (Italy)	1991

SWISS RIDERS

851. Ferdi Kubler
852. 1950
853. Alex Zulle
854. Tony Rominger
855. 3rd (1986)
856. 5
857. 2nd (1993)
858. 2
859. Alex Zulle (1992 & 1996)
860. Tony Rominger

PORTUGUESE RIDERS

861. No Portuguese rider has ever won Le Tour
862. Acacio Da Silva
863. Joaquim Agostinho
864. 10th (1956)
865. Acacio Da Silva (1987-1989)
866. José Azevedo
867. Paulo Ferreira
868. 1
869. Joaquim Agostinho
870. 61st (1992)

COLOMBIAN STAGE WINNERS

871.	Nelson Rodriguez	1994
872.	Santiago Botero	2000
873.	Oliverio Rincon	1993
874.	Luis Herrera	1984

875.	Fabio Parra	1988
876.	Santiago Botero	2002
877.	Pico Gonzalez	1996
878.	Felix Cardenas	2001
879.	Luis Herrera	1985
880.	Fabio Parra	1985

DUTCH PODIUM APPEARANCES

881.	Erik Breukink	1990 (3rd)
882.	Jan Janssen	1968 (1st)
883.	Hennie Kuiper	1980 (2nd)
884.	Steven Rooks	1988 (2nd)
885.	Joop Zoetemelk	1980 (1st)
886.	Peter Winnen	1983 (3rd)
887.	Jan Janssen	1966 (2nd)
888.	Hennie Kuiper	1977 (2nd)
889.	Johan Van der Velde	1982 (3rd)
890.	Joop Zoetemelk	1979 (2nd)

LUXEMBOURG PODIUM APPEARANCES

891.	François Faber	1908 (2nd)
892.	Nicolas Frantz	1928 (1st)
893.	Charly Gaul	1958 (1st)
894.	François Faber	1910 (2nd)
895.	Nicolas Frantz	1926 (2nd)
896.	Charly Gaul	1961 (3rd)
897.	François Faber	1909 (1st)
898.	Nicolas Frantz	1927 (1st)
899.	Charly Gaul	1955 (3rd)
900.	Nicolas Frantz	1924 (2nd)

GERMAN STAGE WINNERS

901.	Olaf Ludwig	1993
902.	Rolf Golz	1988
903.	Jens Voight	2001
904.	Jens Heppner	1998
905.	Rudi Altig	1966
906.	Jan Ullrich	2003
907.	Dietrich Thurau	1979
908.	Erik Zabel	2002
909.	Rolf Wolfshohl	1970

| 910. | Klaus-Peter Thaler | 1978 |

ITALIAN YELLOW JERSEY WEARERS

911.	Flavio Vanzella	1994
912.	Claudio Chiappucci	1990
913.	Marco Pantani	1998
914.	Francesco Moser	1975
915.	Gino Bartali	1937
916.	Ivan Gotti	1995
917.	Fausto Coppi	1952
918.	Gastone Nencini	1960
919.	Alberto Elli	2000
920.	Mario Cipollini	1993

AMERICAN STAGE WINNERS

921.	Greg Lemond	1985
922.	Davis Phinney	1987
923.	Lance Armstrong	1995
924.	Andy Hampsten	1992
925.	Lance Armstrong	2003
926.	Greg Lemond	1989
927.	Tyler Hamilton	2003
928.	Greg Lemond	1986
929.	Lance Armstrong	2004
930.	Jeff Pierce	1987

BELGIAN WINNERS OF LE TOUR

931.	10
932.	4
933.	Firmin Lambot, Sylvere Maes, Eddy Merckx & Philippe Thys
934.	Eddy Merckx (1974)
935.	18
936.	18 (no Belgian rider has ever finished 2nd or 3rd)
937.	2
938.	Philippe Thys (1913, 1914 & 1920)
939.	Peugeot (1913)
940.	Maes (Romain - 1935 & Sylvere - 1936 & 1939)

1996 TOUR DE FRANCE

| 941. | Bjarne Riis |
| 942. | Richard Virenque |

943. Erik Zabel
944. Richard Virenque
945. Festina
946. Jan Ullrich
947. Tony Rominger
948. Fabio Baldato
949. 11th
950. Laurent Dufaux

1995 TOUR DE FRANCE

951. Miguel Indurain
952. Ivan Gotti
953. Laurent Jalabert
954. Richard Virenque
955. Gewiss (Italy)
956. Marco Pantani (1998 Tour de France winner)
957. Melchor Mauri
958. Djamolidin Abdoujaparov
959. 13th
960. Alex Zulle (2nd) & Tony Rominger (8th)

1997 TOUR DE FRANCE

961. Jan Ullrich
962. Marco Pantani
963. Erik Zabel
964. Richard Virenque
965. Telekom
966. Jan Ullrich
967. Abraham Olano
968. Nicola Minali
969. Bobby Julich (17th)
970. Fernando Escartin (5th) & José Maria Jimenez (8th)

GREG LEMOND

971. 3
972. 8
973. 1984
974. 2 (1992 & 1994)
975. 1986
976. Claudio Chiappucci (1990)
977. 5

978.   1985 (Stage 21: Limoges to Lac de Vassivière)
979.   La Vie Claire
980.   5 (1984, 1985, 1986, 1989 & 1990)

SWISS STAGE WINNERS

981.	Rubens Bertogliati	2002
982.	Pascal Richard	1996
983.	Fabian Cancellara	2004
984.	Tony Rominger	1993
985.	Niki Ruttmann	1986
986.	Rolf Jaermann	1992
987.	Alex Zulle	1996
988.	Erich Maechler	1986
989.	Laurent Dufaux	1996
990.	Ferdi Kubler	1954

SPANISH STAGE WINNERS

991.	Fernando Escartin	1999
992.	Juan Miguel Mercado	2004
993.	Miguel Indurain	1992
994.	Iban Mayo	2003
995.	David Etxebarria	1999
996.	Eduardo Chozas	1985
997.	Abraham Olano	1997
998.	Aitor Gonzalez	2004
999.	Carlos Sastre	2003
1000.	Pedro Delgado	1985

FOR THE EXPERT

EXPERT - LE TOUR - 1

1001.   Bernard Hinault (1985)
1002.   It was Le Tour's 100th anniversary
1003.   Luxembourg
1004.   The King of the Mountains Jersey
1005.   25
1006.   60
1007.   François Faber
1008.   It was both the slowest ever Tour and had the fewest number of finishers
1009.   158

1010.   1991

EXPERT - LE TOUR WINNERS - 1

1011.	Bernard Hinault	1978
1012.	Greg Lemond	1989
1013.	Jacques Anquetil	1962
1014.	Bernard Thevenet	1977
1015.	Luis Ocaña	1973
1016.	Roger Pingeon	1967
1017.	Miguel Indurain	1992
1018.	Jan Janssen	1968
1019.	Eddy Merckx	1971
1020.	Felice Gimondi	1965

EXPERT - THE NEARLY MEN 1965 - 1974

1021.	Julio Jimenez	1967
1022.	Felice Gimondi	1972
1023.	Joop Zoetemelk	1970
1024.	Raymond Poulidor	1965
1025.	Bernard Thevenet	1973
1026.	Raymond Poulidor	1974
1027.	Roger Pingeon	1969
1028.	Joop Zoetemelk	1971
1029.	Jan Janssen	1966
1030.	Herman Van Springel	1968

EXPERT - COMBATIVITY WINNERS

1031.	Rik Van Looy (Belgium)	1963
1032.	Raymond Delisle (France)	1976
1033.	Eddy Merckx (Belgium)	1969
1034.	Christian Levavasseur (France)	1980
1035.	Cyrille Guimard (France)	1972
1036.	Désiré Letort (France)	1967
1037.	Gérard Saint (France)	1959
1038.	Luis Ocaña (Spain)	1973
1039.	Felice Gimondi (Italy)	1965
1040.	Roger Pingeon (France)	1968

EXPERT - TOUR RECORDS

| 1041. | Joop Zoetemelk (16: 1970-1986) |
| 1042. | Raymond Poulidor |

1043. 8
1044. Eddy Merckx
1045. Albert Bourlon (France)
1046. Laval to Blois (50.355 km/h: 1999)
1047. Mario Cipollini
1048. Les Sables d'Olonne-Bayonne (1919 & 1924)
1049. 1926 (5,795km over 17 Stages)
1050. Firmin Lambot (Belgium)

EXPERT - RED JERSEY WINNERS

1051.	Gilbert Duclos-Lassalle (France)	1987
1052.	Sean Kelly (Ireland)	1982
1053.	Gerrit Solleveld (Netherlands)	1986
1054.	Jacques Bossis (France)	1978
1055.	Jacques Hanegraaf (Netherlands)	1984
1056.	Pieter Nassen (Belgium)	1971
1057.	Frans Maassen (Netherlands)	1988
1058.	Marc Demeyer (Belgium)	1975
1059.	Freddy Maertens (Belgium)	1981
1060.	Jef Lieckens (Belgium)	1985

EXPERT - ALPE D'HUEZ STAGE WINNERS

1061.	Marco Pantani (Italy)	1997
1062.	Peter Winnen (Netherlands)	1983
1063.	Joop Zoetemelk (Netherlands)	1976
1064.	Fausto Coppi (Italy)	1952
1065.	Gianni Bugno (Italy)	1990
1066.	Peter Winnen (Netherlands)	1981
1067.	Lance Armstrong (USA)	2001
1068.	Hennie Kuiper (Netherlands)	1977
1069.	Gert-Jan Theunisse (Netherlands)	1989
1070.	Beat Breu (Switzerland)	1982

EXPERT - SHORTEST TOURS

1071.	1990	9th
1072.	1905	3rd
1073.	2001	10th
1074.	2003	8th
1075.	1904	Joint 1st
1076.	2002	4th
1077.	2004	7th

1078.	1903	Joint 1st
1079.	1988	5th
1080.	1989	6th

EXPERT - LONGEST TOURS

1081.	1927	9th
1082.	1925	6th
1083.	1920	4th
1084.	1914	8th
1085.	1921	3rd
1086.	1924	7th
1087.	1919	2nd
1088.	1923	10th
1089.	1926	1st
1090.	1928	5th

EXPERT - THE GREEN JERSEY

1091.   Wout Wagtmans (the leader in Points already had the Yellow Jersey)
1092.   1
1093.   Fritz Schär (1953)
1094.   35
1095.   Jean Graczyk, André Darrigade & Laurent Jalabert
1096.   Jan Janssen (1964, 1965 & 1967)
1097.   Stan Ockers
1098.   Jean Forestier
1099.   15
1100.   It was replaced with a red one to placate the "Best Sprinter" sponsor

EXPERT - KING OF THE MOUNTAINS

1101.   Felicien Vervaecke
1102.   1998
1103.   Christophe Rinero
1104.   Julio Jimenez
1105.   Gino Bartali
1106.   Federico Bahamontes (1959)
1107.   Santiago Botero
1108.   Gert-Jan Theunisse
1109.   Gino Bartali (1938 & 1948), Fausto Coppi (1949 & 1952) & Claudio Chiappucci (1991 & 1992)
1110.   Charly Gaul

EXPERT - EDDY MERCKX

1111. 1969
1112. Mulhouse to Ballon d'Alsace (Stage 6: 1969)
1113. Faema
1114. 1969
1115. 6th
1116. 1969 & 1970
1117. 3 (1969, 1971 & 1972)
1118. 1970 & 1974 (he went on to win Le Tour both times)
1119. 1975
1120. 35

EXPERT - TIME TRIAL RECORDS

1121. Gewiss (1995)
1122. 1934 (Stage 22 around Nantes)
1123. US Postal (3rd & 5th)
1124. Switzerland (1954)
1125. Faema (Belgium) (1962)
1126. Coöp-Mercier, Renault, La Vie Claire & Système 'U'
1127. Gerrie Knetemann (50.058 km/h)
1128. Chris Boardman (1994 & 1998)
1129. Raymond Impanis
1130. Raleigh

EXPERT - TOUR WINNERS OF THE 1930s

1131.	André Leducq	1930
1132.	Sylvere Maes	1936
1133.	Roger Lapebie	1937
1134.	Antonin Magne	1934
1135.	Georges Speicher	1933
1136.	Romain Maes	1935
1137.	Antonin Magne	1931
1138.	Sylvere Maes	1939
1139.	André Leducq	1932
1140.	Gino Bartali	1938

EXPERT - LE TOUR - 2

1141. Green
1142. Claudio Chiappucci
1143. Italy (4)
1144. Jacques Anquetil (1961-1964)

1145.   4
1146.   Steven Rooks
1147.   National & Regional Teams replaced the trade-sponsored Teams
1148.   7
1149.   AG2R Prévoyance (France), Brioches la Boulangère (France), Crédit
         Agricole (France), Domina Vacanze (Italy), Lotto-Domo (Belgium), Phonak
         Hearing Systems (Switzerland) & RAGT Semences-MG Rover (France)
1150.   Federico Bahamontes (1959)

EXPERT - WHITE JERSEY WINNERS

1151.	Greg Lemond	1984
1152.	Henk Lubberding	1978
1153.	Laurent Fignon	1983
1154.	Johan Van der Velde	1980
1155.	Benoît Salmon	1999
1156.	Antonio Martín Velasco	1993
1157.	Phil Anderson	1982
1158.	Jan Ullrich	1998
1159.	Francesco Moser	1975
1160.	Peter Winnen	1981

EXPERT - BEST SPRINTERS

1161.	Sean Kelly	1983
1162.	Jan Janssen	1967
1163.	Fritz Schär	1953
1164.	Walter Godefroot	1970
1165.	Willy Planckaert	1966
1166.	Rudi Altig	1962
1167.	Eddy Merckx	1971
1168.	Stan Ockers	1956
1169.	André Darrigade	1961
1170.	Franco Bitossi	1968

EXPERT - JACQUES ANQUETIL

1171.   Felice Gimondi
1172.   Marcel Janssens (1957)
1173.   St-Raphael
1174.   1962, 1963 & 1964
1175.   1957
1176.   4 (1957, 1963 & 1964)
1177.   Raymond Poulidor (1964)

1178.	Rouen (1957)
1179.	1959
1180.	Charly Gaul (1958), Federico Bahamontes (1959) & Gastone Nencini (1960)

EXPERT - TOUR WINNERS - 2

1181.	Lucien Aimar	1966
1182.	Charly Gaul	1958
1183.	Bernard Hinault	1985
1184.	Jacques Anquetil	1963
1185.	Bernard Thevenet	1975
1186.	Louison Bobet	1955
1187.	Gastone Nencini	1960
1188.	Eddy Merckx	1970
1189.	Fausto Coppi	1949
1190.	Lucien Van Impe	1976

EXPERT - LE TOUR "FIRSTS"

1191.	Maurice Garin
1192.	Jacques Anquetil (1957 & 1961-1964)
1193.	Lucien Petit-Breton (1907 & 1908)
1194.	Peugeot (in the 3rd Tour de France of 1905)
1195.	Odile Defraye
1196.	François Faber (1908 & 1909)
1197.	Luxembourg
1198.	Ottavio Bottecchia (1924)
1199.	1915
1200.	Louison Bobet (1953, 1954 & 1955)

EXPERT - THE NEARLY MEN 1975-1984

1201.	Joop Zoetemelk	1976
1202.	Lucien Van Impe	1981
1203.	Joop Zoetemelk	1978
1204.	Bernard Hinault	1984
1205.	Hennie Kuiper	1980
1206.	Angel Arroyo	1983
1207.	Joop Zoetemelk	1979
1208.	Eddy Merckx	1975
1209.	Hennie Kuiper	1977
1210.	Joop Zoetemelk	1982

EXPERT - TIME TRIALS

1211.	Chris Boardman (GB) sets the fastest ever Prologue	1994
1212.	Gewiss (Italy) set the fastest Team Time Trial	1995
1213.	Lance Armstrong (USA) records the 2nd fastest ever time in an Individual Team Time Trial over 30km	2000
1214.	Greg Lemond (USA) sets the fastest ever time in an Individual Team Time Trial between 10-30km	1989
1215.	Fabian Cancellara (Spain) records the 3rd fastest ever Prologue	2004
1216.	Carreras (Italy) set the 2nd record the 2nd fastest ever Team Time Trial	1987
1217.	Chris Boardman (GB) sets the 2nd fastest ever Prologue	1998
1218.	David Millar (GB) sets the fastest ever time in an Individual Team Time Trial over 30km	2003
1219.	Switzerland win the first ever Individual Team Time Trial	1954
1220.	Jan Ullrich (Germany) records the 3rd fastest ever time in an Individual Team Time Trial over 30km	2000

EXPERT - LONGEST SOLO RIDES IN LE TOUR

1221.	Régis Clère (France)	189.5km (9)	1987
1222.	Bernard Quilfen (France)	222km (4)	1977
1223.	Thierry Marie (France)	234km (2)	1991
1224.	Marcel Dussault (France)	200km (7)	1950
1225.	Albert Bourlon (France)	253km (1)	1947
1226.	Fabio Roscioli (Italy)	182.5km (10)	1993
1227.	Pierre Beuffeuil (France)	205km (6)	1966
1228.	José Perez Frances (Spain)	223km (3)	1963
1229.	Roger Pingeon (France)	193km (8)	1968
1230.	Maurice Blomme (Belgium)	214km (5)	1950

EXPERT - TOUR WINNERS OF THE 1950s

1231.	Fausto Coppi	1952
1232.	Jacques Anquetil	1957
1233.	Louison Bobet	1954
1234.	Ferdy Kubler	1950
1235.	Roger Walkowiak	1956
1236.	Louison Bobet	1953
1237.	Federico Bahamontes	1959
1238.	Charly Gaul	1958
1239.	Hugo Koblet	1951
1240.	Louison Bobet	1955

EXPERT - LANCE ARMSTRONG

1241.   1993
1242.   1993, 1994 & 1996
1243.   36th
1244.   Alex Zulle (Switzerland)
1245.   4
1246.   23
1247.   Chalons-sur-Marne to Verdun (Stage 8: 1993)
1248.   2
1249.   1994 & 1996
1250.   Green (Best Sprinter)

Ligettisms:
Favourite Quotes

"He is riding like the halcyon days of Eddy Merckx."
Regarding Lance Armstrong's solo break in the 1995 TdF the day after Casartelli's death.

"He's added another page to this fairy tale that just keeps going on."
1999 TdF after Armstrong won the final Time Trial.

"He's wearing the mask of pain"
Referring to any rider with a grimace (usually suffering up a climb).

"They said this Tour was too short, they said this Tour was too easy (dramatic pause) "THEY....were wrong!!"
From the late 80's, the cameras are showing two pre-race contenders suffering up a climb.

"Having been robbed of the day's prize, you'll notice the big sprinters aren't at the front, sharpening their legs. THEY ONLY LIKE TO WIN - YOU KNOW!!"
Commenting on a slow moving field a few kilometers from the finish. (From the 1995 TdF).

"He's always throwing a spanner into things!"
Commenting on a Chiappucci breakaway.

"There's no reason to rush into hell."
Commenting on a slow moving Paris-Roubaix Peleton.

"Once you pull on that golden fleece, you become two men."
On Wednesday's 17th Sage in the 1996 TdF in reference to Bjarne Riis pulling ahead of the field yet again.

"This is a pedigree group of men, they are holding on by the skin of their shorts."
Regarding the small group of riders who were trying to stay away in Paris on the last day.

"And Brian, I think Sean Kelly told Fignon in broad Irish exactly what he thought of that idea."
From the 1989 World Championships, following Laurent Fignon's gesture for Sean Kelly to go to the front of the chasing group.

"....and Bo Hamburger is, I dare to say it, fried."

"He's ripping the legs off of him."
In regards to Lance Armstrong pulling away from Escartin in the 1999 TdF.

"The peloton is riding like scalded cats."
When Jan Ullrich punctured in the 1997 TdF.

"The pirate is about to board the ship."
When Marco Pantani was catching up with Julich's teammate in the 1998 TdF.

"And Ulrich looks behind him, goodness knows why, because the whole of the Tour de France is in front of him."
Commenting on Jan Ullrich in the 1997 TdF. Ullrich was the last man out, in the ITT.

"They satellite up to eight hours a day to Columbia, waking everybody up on the other side of the world with their persuasive tones."
Referring to the hyperactive Columbian broadcasters in the 1988 TdF (broadcaster practically screaming in the background).

"He looks between his legs and sees.....nobody there!"
For the non-bike racers - a rider on a breakaway will frequently look between his legs to see if someone is chasing as opposed to turning around.

"And Pedro Delgado has sprouted wings!"
1988 TdF. Delgado attacks from a select group of climbers.

"And who is that in the background? That looks like Stephen Roche! IT LOOKS LIKE STEPHEN ROCHE!"
1987 TdF, Delgado arrives at the summit of La Plagne, seemingly having left Roche standing, only for the camera to pick out the Irishman coming back from the dead to finish just a few seconds down.

"To wear the yellow jersey is to mingle with the gods of cycling."

"and now these surgeons of cycling are navigating this rugged French countryside over 'roads made for animals...'"
2000 TdF.

"You can see the fire in Pantani's eyes..." (camera zooms in to reveal the Pirate and he has his Briko sunglasses on).."if it weren't for the sunglasses you could see the fire in his eyes".

"He is, after all, a golden retriever and just doing his job."
2001 Giro d'Italia - commenting on a dog chasing the pack

"Well there you are --never trust a Dutchman!"
1986 TdF. Joel Pelier and Johan Van der Velde have been in a break all day, with the Frenchman doing much of the work, until 100 or so meters from the line when his Dutch companion jumps out from behind to take the Stage victory.

"...and Lance is hanging the pirate on his own ship"
1999 TdF, when Lance Armstrong passes Marco Pantani.

"Every Dag has his day"
Regarding Dag Otto Lauritzen, the 7-11 domestique on winning a TdF Stage.

Sherwenisms:
Favourite Quotes

"And he's popped"
Regarding Lance Armstrong dropping Pantani on Hautecamp - Stage 10, 2000 TdF.

"These riders are glass-cranking it here"
Regarding two breakaway compatriots taking it easy before the finishing sprint - 2000 TdF.

"He probably got a whiff of the alcohol on that man's breath and needed some fresh air."
1997 TdF - Alpe d'Huez when Pantani breaks away dramatically from Ullrich, and as he speeds up the climb, some guy dressed up as a rooster runs up along side him and gets so close that Pantani gives him an elbow.

"Well, I would have climbed off by now. I would never have seen the front this late in the race, but... hills like this were never much to my liking, but..."
Phil asks Paul: "What was it like when you were racing this race?"

"He's really having to dig deeply into the suitcase of courage."
2000 TdF, commenting on Pantani (who was trying to keep the wheel of Lance on the Ventoux).

"As you know, Phil, it is difficult for one Dutchman to outfox another Dutchman"

"He's all over his machine."

"That's what you get when you suffer - you get results."
1999 TdF.

"Would the top of Hautecamp please come quickly."
2000 TdF.